Vocabulary **1**

Games and Activities

New Edition

Vocabulary ❶
Games and Activities
New Edition

Peter Watcyn-Jones

*To the coffee bars in Swansea and Malmö -
a constant source of
inspiration and caffeine-poisoning*

PENGUIN ENGLISH

Pearson Education Limited
Edinburgh Gate
Harlow
Essex CM20 2JE, England
and Associated Companies throughout the world.

ISBN 978-0-582-46566-4

First published 1993
Second impression 2001
This edition published 2001
Copyright © Peter Watcyn-Jones 1993, 2001

9 10

The moral right of the author has been asserted.

Every effort has been made to trace the copyright holders in every case. The publishers would be interested to hear from any not acknowledged.

Designed and typeset by Ferdinand Pageworks
Illustrations by Mark Davis, Jean de Lemos and Ross Thomson
Printed in China   SWTC/09

Published by Pearson Education Limited in association with Penguin Books Ltd, both companies being subsidiaries of Pearson plc.

For a complete list of the titles available from Penguin English
please write to your local Pearson Education office or to:
Marketing Department, Pearson Education, Edinburgh Gate, Harlow, Essex CM20 2JE

Contents

Key to contents table			
Activity type		**Preparation**	
👤	individual	📄	1 handout to copy
👥	pair work	📄	several handouts to copy
👨‍👩‍👧	group work	✂️📄	1 handout to copy and cut up
👨‍👩‍👧‍👦	whole class activity	✂️📄	several handouts to copy and cut up
🎓	teacher-led activity	✂️📄	handout to be cut up into several pieces or into cards

Game/Activity	Time	Key vocabulary/Topic	Activity type	Preparation	Pages
11 Pairwork cards: Clothes	30 mins	Things people wear (Clothes & accessories): *coat, shoes, gloves, socks, hat, shirt, watch, ring, etc.*	👫	📄 ✂️🗒️	7/71–72
12 Complete the sentences	20 mins	Various nouns, verbs and adjectives: *umbrella, daughter, birthday, hungry, cheap, borrow, spell, etc.*	🎓	📄 ✂️🗒️	7/73/156

Elementary/Pre-intermediate

Game/Activity	Time	Key vocabulary/Topic	Activity type	Preparation	Pages
13 Find someone who … 1	20 mins	Various words	👨‍👩‍👧‍👦	📄	9/74
14 The alphabet race	15 mins	Letters of the alphabet; ordinal numbers: *first, second, fifteenth, etc.*	👫	📄	9/75
15 Bingo: Opposites	10 mins per game	Opposites (adjectives): *big–small; weak–strong; dry–wet; fast–slow, etc.*	🎓	✂️🗒️ ✂️🗒️	10/76–78
16 Matching pairs: Verbs + noun collocations	25 mins	Verb + noun collocations: *answer the phone, ask a question, brush your teeth, etc.*	👫	✂️🗒️	11/79–80
17 Matching pairs: More mini dialogues	20 mins	2-line exchanges: *It's my birthday today. Many happy returns! etc.*	👫	✂️🗒️	11/81–82
18 Dominoes: Compound nouns 2	20 mins	Compound nouns: *ashtray, basketball, bedroom, briefcase, etc.*	👨‍👩‍👦	✂️🗒️	12/83–84
19 Half a crossword: Sports, hobbies and pastimes	30 mins	Sports, hobbies and pastimes: *athletics, badminton, camping, yoga, etc.*	👨‍👩‍👦	📄	13/85–86
20 Half a crossword: Useful verbs	30–35 mins	Verbs: *cry, drive, run, dance, phone, etc.*	👨‍👩‍👦	📄	13/87–88
21 Group the words 2: Nouns	20 mins	Various nouns grouped under headings: **In the kitchen** *cooker, fridge, frying pan, microwave* **In the bathroom** *shower, soap, etc.*	👨‍👩‍👦	✂️🗒️	14/89
22 Complete the story	20 mins	Various nouns, verbs adverbs and adjectives: *wished, journey, exactly, disappointed, wife, etc.*	🎓	📄 ✂️🗒️	15/90/156
23 Word association maze	10 mins	Various nouns which can be associated with each other: *letter–envelope, bird–nest, husband–wife, etc.*	👫	📄	16/91
24 Vocabulary quiz: Food, shops and shopping	30 mins	Food, shops and shopping vocabulary: *breakfast, grape, cucumber, a bottle of, chef, florist, loaf, etc.*	👨‍👩‍👧‍👦	📄	17/92–93

Introduction

Vocabulary Games and Activities 1 is a source book for teachers, containing a collection of sixty games and activities for teaching and revising vocabulary. They range from elementary to advanced activities, the majority of which contain material to be photocopied. It is hoped they will provide useful extra material which will be of interest to most students and show that vocabulary learning can be both interesting and fun.

The lexical items in the book have been carefully chosen, with many words taken from the author's *Test Your Vocabulary* and *Target Vocabulary* series (also published by Penguin Books). In addition, where possible many words are recycled in different exercises. Activities invariably have to be changed or adapted to suit one's own particular group of students, so I hope teachers will feel free to make any changes they feel necessary. What is presented in **Vocabulary Games and Activities 1** is, to a large extent, ideas which I hope will stimulate and encourage teachers to devise their own activities based on these ideas.

I am sometimes asked why one should go to the trouble of photocopying and cutting out words for activities when the same thing could probably be done on a single sheet of paper. My answer is that although it is certainly more work for the teacher, the results are well worth it. Learning seems to become more active, the students get more involved and, in my experience, retention improves enormously. Once a student has done an exercise on paper, it feels 'finished' and is never easy to repeat. By allowing the students to physically arrange words on a table (e.g. in matching pairs or grouping of words), the sense of touch is used, and the more senses that are involved in the learning process the better. The learning process is also made more dynamic and enjoyable by working with fellow-students, and most of the activities in this book are designed for pair work, group work and, occasionally, as whole class activities.

Finally, it is always difficult to know which ideas can be claimed as one's own and which are other people's. Where I have consciously used someone else's idea I have of course acknowledged this. In other cases where I have devised an activity which someone else can lay prior claim to (it is possible for two people to come up with the same idea quite independently) then I apologise and will gladly make the appropriate acknowledgement in future editions of this book.

The organisation of this book

The activities have been grouped into five sections according to level:

1   Beginner/Elementary
2   Elementary/Pre-intermediate
3   Pre-intermediate/Intermediate
4   Intermediate/Upper Intermediate
5   Upper Intermediate/Advanced

Each level contains twelve games and activities. These are varied and include Ice-breaker activities, Bingo activities, Matching pairs activities, Crossword and Word square activities, Pairwork and Board games, Teacher-led activities, etc.

Detailed teacher's notes are given for each activity. These include notes and explanations of words which the students may have trouble with. A key is also given, where appropriate.

Finally, at the back of the book is a list of all the key, words found in the book.

Classroom organisation

Although class sizes vary considerably, the book assumes an average class size of 10–20 students. Where possible, the classroom should be physically rearranged to facilitate working in pairs or groups. However, should this not be possible, even the more traditional front-facing rows of desks can be easily adapted for pairwork and group work. For pairwork, students can either work with the person sitting next to them or the person in front of or behind them. For group work, two students can easily turn their chairs round to face two others behind them.

Where you have an uneven number of students in the class, most pairwork activities can be done by three people (if necessary, two students against one).

The role of the teacher

Apart from the activities in the section *Teacher-led activities*, the teacher's role is largely a passive one. The teacher is mainly responsible for:

* preparing the material in sufficient quantities

* explaining clearly what is to be done

* 'checking' answers at the end of an activity.

Once an activity has started, students usually work independently of the teacher at their own pace. The teacher goes round the classroom listening and monitoring their progress and only interfering or helping if *absolutely necessary*.

Note for busy teachers

Teachers are often very busy and there is not always a lot of time for preparation, especially when it involves both copying and cutting up handouts onto cards, etc. If this is the case, several of the activities in this book can still be used (though obviously not as effectively). In particular the following:

Matching pair activities (Nos 4, 5, 16, 17, 27, 28, 39 & 55). The sheets can be given out and can be matched up on paper.

Domino activities (Nos 7, 18, 29, 40). The board and domino sheet can be given out and the words (on the dominoes) written onto the board instead of them being placed around it.

Group the words (Nos 9, 21, 45). The handouts can be given out and the students write the words under each heading on a separate piece of paper.

Complete the sentences/story activities (Nos 12, 22). The handouts (board and card) can be given out and instead of placing each word on the number sheet, the students write them in.

Time-limits

A suggested time-limit is given for each activity. However, this can vary depending on the group. For this reason I strongly advise giving the class a time-limit for most of the activities, and to stop them whether they have finished or not. Apart from the obvious difficulties of students finishing at different times, the checking process is often an integral and, from the learning point of view, an important part of the activity. As such it is better that you check with the whole class rather than individual groups.

Storing the material

The material to be photocopied can be divided into two types: (a) handouts which the students write on, and (b) material which the students use but do not write on.

To save the teacher unnecessary work, therefore, it is a good idea that material that can be re-used is made as durable as possible. One way is to mount everything on thin card. (Many photocopiers nowadays allow the use of card.) These cards and handouts can then be laminated and stored in separate envelopes (clearly labelled on the outside) which can be handed back to the teacher at the end of the activity.

Nearly all the activities presented in this book require preparation on the part of the teacher. (The amount of preparation required is clearly indicated in the contents.) It is hoped that all the extra effort will prove to be rewarding.

Part 1: **Teacher's notes**

Beginner/Elementary

1 Find the words

Time: 20 minutes

Type of activity: Ice-breaker activity for the whole class (twenty students) – especially useful with a new class where the students still haven't learnt each others' names.

Preparation: Copy the handout on page 49 – one copy for each student. Also copy and cut up the word cards on pages 50–51 – one for each student. *

Lexical area/Topic
Various nouns
an ashtray, a bag, a biscuit, a carrot, a chicken, a chimney, a dentist, a desk, a door, an envelope, a horse, a knife, a pig, a saucepan, a sausage, a shop assistant, a spoon, an umbrella, a vase, a watch

Method

1 Give each student a copy of the main handout. Also give each student an individual word card.

2 Give them time to read through the card and ask you about anything they do not understand. Also make sure that they can pronounce the word and, if necessary, spell it.

3 Tell them to write the word on their handout next to the correct drawing.

4 The students then stand up and walk around the room. Every time they meet someone they tell them the word they were given, plus their name. (The other person writes both down next to the correct drawing).

5 After a while (approximately 15 mins.), stop the activity whether or not everybody has managed to fill in all twenty words.

6 Finally, go through all the drawings orally, asking random students to tell you what it is and who told them.

* NOTE: If there are fewer than twenty students in the class, give some students more than one card. They then read out both cards when they meet someone.
If there are more than twenty students in the class, then some cards will have to be duplicated.

2 Bingo: Useful verbs

Time: 10 minutes per game

Type of activity: Teacher-led picture bingo activity, with the students working individually (or in pairs in larger classes).

Preparation: Copy the eight students' cards on pages 53–54 and cut them out – one card per student (or per pair if the class is large). If you plan to play the game twice, give each student two cards to start with. Also make one copy of the teacher's handout on page 52. (You will need to cut out the bottom half into small squares.)

Lexical area/Topic
Useful 'action' verbs
climb, cook, cry, dance, drink, drive, eat, jump, kick, laugh, phone, read, run, sing, sleep, swim

Method

1 Give out the bingo cards. Allow the students a few minutes to look through them before beginning. (If the class is large, students work in pairs.)

2 Put the sixteen squares you have cut up into some kind of container (hat, cup, etc.) and draw them out one at a time. Say the name on the square and place it on your 'Master board'. If the students have the word (a picture on their cards), they cross it out.

3 Continue until a student has crossed out every picture, in which case s/he shouts out *Bingo*!

4   Now you stop the game and ask the student to say the six verbs on his/her card that s/he has crossed out. (You can ask another student to monitor this, to avoid any cheating!) Check on your board that these verbs have been called out.

5   If a mistake has been made, continue with the game until someone wins.

6   You can then play again with different cards. You might even ask one of the students to be the caller!

3   Bingo: Things in the home

Time: 10 minutes per game
Type of activity: Teacher-led picture bingo activity, with the students working individually (or in pairs in larger classes).
Preparation: Copy the eight students' cards on pages 56–57 and cut them out – one card per student (or per pair if the class is large). If you plan to play the game twice, give each student two cards to start with. Also make one copy of the teacher's handout on page 55. (You will need to cut out the bottom half into small squares.)

Lexical area/Topic
Things in the home
bed, book, bottle, camera, chair, clock, cup, glass, knife, lamp, plate, spoon, table, telephone, television, umbrella

Method

As Activity 2 above.

4   Matching pairs: My day

Time: 25 minutes
Type of activity: Pairwork activity, based on matching the correct verb (A-cards) with the correct drawing (B-cards) and then arranging them in the most logical order.
Preparation: Copy and cut up the verb cards (A) and the drawings (B) on pages 58–59 – one set for each pair/group, plus one set of B-cards for yourself.

Lexical area/Topic
Verbs to describe daily routines
wake up, switch off the alarm clock, get up, go to the bathroom, brush my teeth, have a shower, have breakfast, read the newspaper, drive to work, have lunch, come home, read my mail, make dinner, watch TV, go to bed, set the alarm clock, read in bed, switch off the light, fall asleep, dream

Method

1   Divide the class into pairs (or groups of three). Give each pair a set of A- and B-cards.

2   Tell them they have to arrange them into twenty pairs of words comprising an action (on the left) and a drawing (on the right). Tell them they also have to decide on a 'correct' or 'logical' order in which you would do these actions during a normal day.

3   Allow 15 minutes for this. Go round and check that the pairs/groups have matched up the drawings correctly.

4   Check orally with the whole class. Do it this way. Shuffle the drawings (B-cards) and hold them up one at a time. Ask different pairs/groups to give you the corresponding verbs. Next, ask one pair/group to give you their 'daily' sequence. Write it up on the board. Ask the others in the class if there's anything they disagree with. Encourage discussion, since there is more than one 'correct' answer.

Key (also suggested 'correct' sequence)

wake up – 6, switch off the alarm clock – 13, get up – 7, go to the bathroom – 16, brush my teeth – 8, have a shower – 19, have breakfast – 1, read the newspaper – 18, drive to work – 2, have lunch – 14, come home – 9, read my mail –12, make dinner – 3, watch TV – 15, go to bed – 4, set the alarm clock – 10, read in bed – 17, switch off the light – 5, fall asleep – 20, dream – 11

5 Matching pairs: Mini dialogues

Time: 20 minutes

Type of activity: Pairwork activity, based on matching 2-line mini dialogues.

Preparation: Copy and cut up the opening words (A) and the replies (B) on pages 60–61 – one set for each pair/group, plus one set of A-cards for yourself.

Lexical area/Topic
Various useful responses and answers
Hello. How are you? I'm fine, thanks.
What's your name? It's Steve … Steve Brown.
I've just got married! Congratulations! etc.

Method

1 Divide the class into pairs (or groups of three). Give each pair a set of A- and B-cards.

2 Tell them they have to arrange them into twelve mini dialogues, with the opening words (on the left) and the replies (on the right). Point out that the reply cards are numbered 1–12.

3 Allow 15 minutes for this. Go round and help, if necessary with vocabulary.

4 Check orally with the whole class. Do it this way. Shuffle the opening words (A-cards) and hold them up one at a time. Ask different pairs/groups to give you the corresponding reply.

Follow-up activity

1 Students work in pairs – A and B. One student (A) has all the A-cards, the other student (B) has the B-cards.

2 Student B places his/her face up in front of him/her.

3 Student A shuffles his/her and places them face down on the table. S/He takes up the top card and reads it out. Student B tries to reply with the correct response. If s/he does, the card is turned over. If not, Student A can guess the answer and 'claim' the card. If no one knows the answer,

Student A places the card at the bottom of the pile, to be used later on.

4 Continue in this way until all the cards have been used up.

5 If time, the students change roles and do it again.

NOTE: To make it more difficult, see if Student B can answer *without* looking at the B-cards.

Key to cards

Hello. How are you? (5); What's your name? (11); How old are you? (1); I've just got married. (7); I'm sorry I'm late. (9); Where do you live? (4); Are you English? (2); Can you help me, please? (10); Would you like a cigarette? (6); What's the date today? (12); Have a nice weekend. (3); Thank you for helping me. (8)

6 Dominoes: Food words

Time: 20 minutes

Type of activity: Group activity, based on the game of dominoes, where the students have to match food words with the correct drawings to fit all the dominoes on the board.

Preparation: Copy the domino board on page 62 – one board per group. Also copy and cut up the dominoes on page 63 – again, one set per group. Only cut where there is a dashed line. You should not cut along solid lines.

Lexical area/Topic
Various food words
apple, banana, bread, cake, cheese, chocolate, egg, fish, French fries (chips), hamburger, ice-cream, meat, orange, pizza, rice, sandwich, tomato

Method

1 Divide the class into groups of 3–4. Give each group a board and a set of dominoes.

2 Point out that the board already contains one domino – namely above the words **Start here**. If you like, ask them if they

know what the drawing is. *(French fries or chips)*

3   Tell them that they have to place the remainder of the dominoes on the board in such a way that picture–word combinations are formed by combining the right-hand word of one domino with the left-hand picture of the one next to it.

4   Allow 15 minutes for this. Go round and help, if necessary, with vocabulary.

5   Check by beginning with the first domino *French fries (chips): apple.* Continue in a clockwise direction until you end with *rice: French fries (chips).*

Acknowledgement:
This is based on an idea from *Word Games With English Plus* by Deirdre Howard-Williams and Cynthia Herd, Heinemann 1989, p. 8.

Key

The correct order (clockwise) is:

apple: banana; banana: cake; cake: ice-cream; ice-cream: bread; bread: orange; orange: pizza; pizza: hamburger; hamburger: tomato; tomato: sandwich; sandwich: egg; egg: cheese; cheese: fish; fish: meat; meat: chocolate; chocolate: rice, rice; French fries (chips)

7   Dominoes: Compound nouns 1

Time: 20 minutes
Type of activity: Group activity, based on the game of dominoes, where the students have to make compound nouns and thus fit all the dominoes on the board.
Preparation: Copy the domino board on page 64 – one board per group. Also copy and cut up the dominoes on page 65 – again, one set per group. Be careful only to cut along the dashed lines. Do not cut along the solid lines.

Lexical area/Topic
Compound nouns
alarm clock, armchair, bathroom, bookcase, car park, cupboard, football, homework, newspaper,

phone box, police officer, postcard, raincoat, suitcase, sunglasses, toothbrush, washing machine

Method

As Activity 6 above. Before starting, point out that the board already contains one domino, namely *officer: washing.* Also point out that the drawings in the middle of the board are the words they have to find.

Key (dominoes)

The correct order (clockwise) is:

officer: washing; machine: bath; room: car; park: home; work: book; case: arm; chair: suit; case: alarm; clock: sun; glasses: tooth; brush: foot; ball: rain; coat: news; paper: phone; box: post; card: cup; board: police

8   Half a crossword: Jobs and people

Time: 30 minutes
Type of activity: Group activity, based on a crossword. Each group has an incomplete crossword. By asking for and giving definitions, they try to fill in the missing words.
Preparation: Copy the crossword on page 66 (for Group A students) and on page 67 (for Group B students).

Lexical area/Topic
Jobs and people
actor, boss, brother, bus driver, dentist, doctor, friend, girl, hairdresser, husband, mother, neighbour, nurse, parents, police officer, student, teacher, waiter

Method

1   Before starting, it might be a good idea to revise with the groups ways of defining people. Write the following on the board:

> *It's someone who …*
> *It's a person who …*
> *It's a man/woman who …*
> *This person works …*
> *This person wears (a uniform).*
> *He/She is your …*

Write up the word **soldier** on the board. Ask student to suggest a way of explaining what a soldier is. *(e.g. He wears a uniform. It's someone who fights for his country.)*

Then write up the word **uncle**. Again ask for suggestions for how to describe it. *(e.g. He's your mother's brother. He's your father's brother.)*

Keep the phrases on the board, so the students can have them for reference.

2 Divide the class into A and B groups of between 2–4 students per group. They sit facing each other. Give each group the appropriate crossword and allow them time to check through the words they will need to define before starting. If necessary, give individual help at this stage.

NOTE: On no account must they allow the other group to see their crossword.

3 Explain that they have to take it in turns to ask for a word that is missing from their crossword. They simply ask: *What's 3 down? What's 14 across?*, etc. The other group now try to give as clear a definition as possible to help them guess the word.

4 Set a definite time-limit (e.g. 25 mins.) and stop the students at the end of it, *whether they have finished or not.*

5 They can now compare crosswords and check any words they didn't fill in.

6 You can follow up by asking the groups to explain how they defined one or two words from the crossword.

Acknowledgement:
This is based on an idea by Elizabeth Woodeson, which appeared in *Modern English Teacher*, Vol. 10, 1982.

9 Group the words 1: Nouns

Time: 20 minutes
Type of activity: Group activity, based on placing the correct nouns under the correct headings.
Preparation: Copy and cut up the cards on page 68 – one set per group.

Lexical area/Topic
Word groups (various nouns)
Relatives
aunt, cousin, grandparents, uncle
Buildings
department store, hospital, hotel, post office
Transport
aeroplane (plane), bicycle (bike), bus, car
Parts of the body
ear, finger, mouth, nose

Method

1 Divide the class into groups of 4–5. Give each group a set of words. Do **not** hand out the headings yet!

2 Tell them they have to arrange the words into groups of four – where each word is linked in some way. (They will need a desk or table on which to work.)

3 Allow 10–12 minutes for this. Then give out the headings. Tell them that these are the headings the words should be arranged under. Allow 5 more minutes for them to complete the task.

5 Instead of just reading out the correct answers at the end, you might like to try the following:

Ask one group to tell you which words they have placed under *RELATIVES*. If they didn't get them all right, tell them which words are correct, e.g. *You got three right – aunt, cousin and grandparents.*
Move on to the next group and ask them if they can say what the missing word is. Continue in this way until all four words are given. (In the unlikely event that after going round the class you still haven't found four correct words, tell them the answer.)

Continue in this way with the remaining three groups. (By using this method of checking, it allows the groups to 'change their minds' and reshuffle their cards during the checking stage.)

Key

Relatives: *aunt, cousin, grandparents, uncle;*
Buildings: *department store, hospital, hotel, post office;* **Transport:** *aeroplane (plane), bicycle (bike), bus, car;* **Parts of the body:** *ear, finger, mouth, nose*

10 Board game: Categories 1

Time: 20–25 minutes
Type of activity: Board game for two teams, based on placing words correctly according to which category they belong to. There are ten categories altogether with four words per category.
Preparation: Copy the playing board on page 69 – one board per group (of two teams). Also copy the sheet of words on page 70 – one per team.

Lexical area/Topic
Word groups
Jobs
dentist, secretary, shop assistant, teacher
Furniture
bed, bookcase, chair, table
Colours
black, blue, green, yellow
Fruit
apple, banana, pear, strawberry
Vegetables
carrot, cucumber, onion, potato
Parts of the body
back, foot, leg, toe
Action verbs
climb, dance, swim, throw
Things in a town
bridge, bus stop, cinema, street
Adjectives to describe people
beautiful, friendly, happy, intelligent
Things in the home
clock, lamp, radio, telephone (phone)

Method

1   Divide the class into groups of four. Further divide each group into two teams –

A and B. Give each team a copy of the board, plus a copy of the sheet of words.

2   If necessary, before they start, demonstrate with the whole class so they understand what they have to do. Write the following two headings on the board:

CLOTHES   SMALL OBJECTS

Make sure they understand the headings, then write the following word on the board: *spoon*
Choose one group to demonstrate with. Ask the A team to suggest which heading the word 'spoon' should go under. Write down their answer (whether it is correct or not) under the appropriate heading. Also add the letter A after it, to show which team has answered.
Continue with the following words, asking alternate teams for the answer:
key, coin, tie, vest, paper clip, trainers, coat
When all the words have been placed, go through orally. Award 1 point for each correct answer. (CLOTHES: *tie, vest, trainers, coat;* SMALL OBJECTS: *spoon, key, coin, paper clip*) Which team won – A or B?

3   Explain that they have to do the same now but with ten categories instead of two. They take it in turns to choose a word from the word sheet, then to write the word under one of the categories, not forgetting to write A or B after the word so they know who wrote it at the end. At the same time both teams now cross out that word from the word sheet. Tell them that there should be four words under each category. Also tell them **not** to tell their opponents if they see that they have written the word under the wrong category because, at the end, they will score 1 point for each correct answer and deduct 1 point for each incorrect one! Also tell them that they can write more than four words under each heading, but that only four will be correct when they check! (This is to enable a team to put a word under the correct heading when their opponent has wrongly placed a word there.)

4   Allow approximately 20 minutes for this. Then stop everyone whether or not they have placed all the words.

5   Check orally with the whole class. Read out the headings and invite answers. Say which four words are correct and tell them that they score 1 point for each word they placed correctly and deduct 1 point for each word in the wrong place!

6   The teams add up their scores. Check which team – A or B – won in each group. Also see who had the highest score in the class.

Key

Jobs: *dentist, secretary, shop assistant, teacher;*
Furniture: *bed, bookcase, chair, table;* **Colours:** *black, blue, green, yellow;* **Fruit:** *apple, banana, pear, strawberry;* **Vegetables:** *carrot, cucumber, onion, potato;* **Parts of the body:** *back, foot, leg, toe;* **Action verbs:** *climb, dance, swim, throw;* **Things in a town:** *bridge, bus stop, cinema, street;* **Adjectives to describe people:** *beautiful, friendly, happy, intelligent;* **Things in the home:** *clock, lamp, radio, telephone (phone)*

11 Pairwork cards: Clothes, etc.

Time: 30 minutes
Type of activity: Pairwork card activity, where the students test each other on clothes words. There are four cards altogether. Each card has a front (A) and a back (B). On the front are drawings only of five items of clothing/accessories. On the back are both drawings and what they are called. Student B asks Student A to recognise the words s/he says by saying which drawing it is. This is a simple but effective way of teaching and testing words.
Preparation: Copy the four pairwork cards on pages 71–72 – one complete set for each pair.

Lexical area/Topic
Things people wear (clothes and accessories)

belt, boots, coat, dress, glasses, gloves, hat, jacket, jeans, jumper, ring, shirt, shoes, shorts, socks, T-shirt, tights, trainers, trousers, watch

Method

1   Divide the class into pairs – A and B. Give each pair a set of cards. Before giving out the cards, fold them in half and tape the ends. (Alternatively, stick each half onto either side of a piece of card.)

2   Students decide who is going to ask and who is going to answer first. The student who is going to ask (e.g. Student B) takes charge of the four cards. The basic method of working with each card is as follows: (Demonstrate with one of the students first, if necessary.)

The card is held up so that Student (A) can only see the drawings. Student (B) now reads out (in any order) one of the five questions. (Remind the students that we use *is* with singular words and *are* with plural words.) e.g.
Which number is the (hat)?
Student (A) looks at the five drawings and gives an answer, e.g. *It's number 3.*
Student (B) knows if the answer is right or wrong because the 'correct' answer (*It's number 3.*) is given after each word. So s/he answers, *Yes, that's right.* or *No, that's wrong. It's number x.*
Continue like this with the remaining four drawings.
When all four cards have been gone through, tell the students to change roles and do it again. (It should be a lot easier for the student who goes second!)

12 Complete the sentences

Time: 20 minutes
Type of activity: Teacher-led whole class activity with the students working in small groups of three. The teacher reads out twenty sentences with gaps and the students have to decide which word is missing in each sentence.

Preparation: Copy the *Numbers 1–20* sheet on page 156 – one copy per group. Also copy and cut up the cards on page 73 – again, one set per group.

Lexical area/Topic
Various nouns, verbs and adjectives
Nouns
address, birthday, capital, cat, daughter, department store, doctor, floor, foreigner, ring, snow, umbrella
Verbs
borrow, invite, smile, spell
Adjectives
blonde, cheap, dirty, hungry

Method

1   Divide the class into groups of 3–4 per group. Give each group a copy of the *Numbers 1–20* sheet plus a set of cards. Tell the students to arrange the cards on the desk in front of them. Try to get them to arrange them into nouns, verbs and adjectives. Allow 5 minutes for this. Go around and check that they understand the words.

2   Read out the sentences below, one at a time. Say the number of the sentence *before* you read it out. If necessary, read each sentence more than once. Make sure you clearly indicate (by making a sound, etc.) where the missing word is in each sentence.

3   The students look at their words and decide if they can find one which will fit into the sentence you have just read out. They place it in box 1 for sentence 1, box 2 for sentence 2, and so on. Encourage them to guess, even if they aren't 100 per cent sure.

4   Continue in this manner until you have read out all twenty sentences.

5   Check orally. Ask for suggestions for each missing word before reading out the sentence again. Give each group 1 point for each correct answer.

6   Which group scored the most?

Follow-up

The students shuffle their cards and place them face down on the table in front of them. They now spread them out like a pack of cards and pick out five at random. Working together, they try to write their own gapped sentence for these cards. Get them to read out their sentences. The rest of the class listen and try to guess what the missing words are.

Sentences (to be read out by the teacher)

Don't forget to say the number of the sentence *before* you read it. And also to remind the students where to put their words. (See sentence 1 for example.) The answers are given in **bold type** after each sentence. (Don't read them out yet!)

1   Say: *This is sentence number 1 … sentence number 1. Listen and then try to guess which word is missing.*
It's raining. You'd better take an ___(bleep!)___ with you. **umbrella**
So which word is missing? Don't tell anyone! Just put it in box number 1.
(Continue like this.)

2   My sister has two children, a boy and a girl. Her son is called Mark and her ___(bleep!)___ is called Amanda. **daughter**

3   Which animal would you like as a pet – a ___(bleep!)___ or a dog? **cat**

4   She was a beautiful and famous film star, with blue eyes and long ___(bleep!)___ hair. **blonde**

5   I never buy books. I always ___(bleep!)___ them from the library instead. **borrow**

6   He isn't from this country. He's a ___(bleep!)___. **foreigner**

7   It's Paul's ___(bleep!)___ on Saturday. She's 17. Are you going to her party? **birthday**

8   'How do you ___(bleep!)___ strawberry?' 'S–T–R–A–W–B–E double R–Y.' **spell**

9   See that block of flats over there? My grandparents live there. They've got a

small flat on the second ___(bleep!)___.
floor

10 The dress was really ___(bleep!)___. It only cost £10. **cheap**

11 Where do you live? What's your ___(bleep!)___? **address**

12 Peter and I have just got married. Would you like to see my wedding ___(bleep!)___? **ring**

13 *Harrods* is a very famous ___(bleep!)___ in London. **department store**

14 He was feeling ill, so he went to see a ___(bleep!)___. **doctor**

15 Let's have something to eat. I feel really ___(bleep!)___! **hungry**

16 Copenhagen is the ___(bleep!)___ of Denmark. **capital**

17 How many people shall we ___(bleep!)___ to the party on Saturday? **invite**

18 In Canada they get a lot of ___(bleep!)___ in the winter. **snow**

19 ___(bleep!)___ everybody! And look at the camera! **smile**

20 Wash your hands before you have dinner! They're really ___(bleep!)___! **dirty**

Elementary – Pre-intermediate

13 Find someone who ... 1

Time: 20 minutes
Type of activity: Ice-breaker activity for the whole class.
Preparation: Copy the handout on page 74 – one copy for each student.

Lexical area/Topic
Various words

Method

1 Give each student a copy of the handout.

2 Give them time to read through the questions and ask you about anything they do not understand.

3 The students then stand up and walk around the room trying to find answers to the questions on their handout. To ensure that they talk to as many people as possible, tell them that they are only allowed to ask two questions every time they talk to someone.

4 They write down any answers to their questions, plus the name of the student who gave them the answer.

5 After a while (approximately 15 mins.), stop the activity and have a whole class feedback. Go through all the questions orally, asking random students to read out any answers they got for each one.

Key (suggestion only)

1 Choose two from: apple, orange, pear, grapefruit, banana, grapes, strawberry, peach, etc.; 2 Choose two from: cabbage, potato, peas, carrot, cucumber, tomato, leek, onion, etc.; 3 poor, small, young; 4 cakes, bread (bakery); meat, sausages, chicken (butcher); 5 a spider; 6 Choose from: red, orange, yellow, green, blue, indigo, violet; 7 Choose two from: kitchen (sink, cooker, saucepan, spoon, cupboard, fridge, etc.); bathroom (bath, shower, sink, soap, shampoo, toothbrush, toothpaste, toilet, etc.); bedroom (bed, wardrobe, lamp, pillow, sheet, blanket, etc.); 8 money, credit cards, etc.; 9 Choose three from: tea, coffee, water, milk, wine, beer, whisky, gin, vodka, orange juice, Coca-Cola (Coke), etc.; 10 Free choice (e.g. hamburger, pizza, fish and chips, spaghetti, etc.); 11 umbrella; 12 Choose three from: England, Scotland, Wales, France, Spain, Portugal, Italy, Germany, Ireland, Holland, Sweden, Denmark, Finland, Norway, Belgium, Switzerland, Austria, etc.; 13 Choose three from: cat, dog, horse, lion, elephant, mouse, bull, cow, etc.; 14 men (coat, shirt, trousers, tie, jeans, suit, jacket, jumper, T-shirt, etc.)
women: (dress, skirt, tights, blouse, socks, bra, etc.); 15 doctor

14 The alphabet race

Time: 20 minutes
Type of activity: Warm-up pairwork activity based on the alphabet. (Useful for

students whose language has a different alphabet.)

Preparation: Copy the handout on page 75 – one copy for each pair.

Lexical area/Topic

The letters of the alphabet

Ordinal numbers, plus words that start or end with certain letters of the alphabet

Method

1   Divide the class into pairs. Give each pair a copy of the handout.

2   Go through the alphabet orally to check the students can pronounce the various letters. Ask random questions, e.g. *Which letter comes after S? What's the last letter of the alphabet? Which letter comes before V? How many vowels are there? What are they? What's a consonant? Name two. Is F a vowel or a consonant? Can you think of a word beginning with the third letter of the alphabet? (cat) Can you think of a word that ends with the fourth letter of the alphabet? (word)* etc.

3   When everyone is ready, tell them to begin. After 10 minutes tell them to stop. Get the pairs to change papers and to mark each other's answers.

4   Check orally, by asking different pairs for their answers. Award 1 point for each correct answer.

5   The students hand their papers back to each other. Which pair scored the most?

Key

1 N (1 point); 2 T (1 point); 3 (the letter D) dog, day, etc. (2 points); 4 BOAT (1 point); 5 seven (D–I–F–E–R–N–T) (1 point); 6 (the letter R) car, hair, etc. (2 points); 7 E, L, H, N (4 points); 8 T (1 point); 9 A (1 point); 10 (V) 2 (I, E): (C) 5 (N, T, R, S, G) (2 points); 11 15th/fifteenth (1 point); 12 J (1 point); 13 card, carrot, comb, coffee, cream (5 points); 14 R (1 point); 15 (the letters C and P) cap, cup, etc. (1 point) TOTAL SCORE = 25 points

15 Bingo: Opposites

Time: 10 minutes per game

Type of activity: Teacher-led bingo activity based on opposites (adjectives), with the students working individually (or in pairs in larger classes).

Preparation: Copy the eight students' cards on pages 77–78 and cut them out – one card per student (or per pair if the class is large). If you plan to play the game twice, give each student two cards to start with. Also make one copy of the teacher's handout on page 76. (You will need to cut out the bottom half into small squares.)

Lexical area/Topic

Opposites

big – small; weak – strong; dry – wet; fast – slow; clean – dirty; happy – sad; hard – soft; hot – cold; light – heavy; good – bad; low – high; old – young; rich – poor; right – wrong; tall – short; fat – thin

Method

1   If you think your students already know these opposites, go on to 2. If not, before starting, choose random pairs and ask them for one of the words on their cards, e.g. *big.* Ask anyone if they know what the opposite of *big* is? *(small)* Continue like this with the other adjectives. Alternatively, you could write on the board all the words in brackets on your 'Master board'. Then go through them one by one, asking the students to say if they have a word on their card that is opposite in meaning to the word on the board.

2   Give out the bingo cards. Allow the students a few minutes to look through them before beginning. (If the class is large, students work in pairs.)

3   Put the sixteen squares you have cut up into some kind of container (hat, cup, etc.) and draw them out one at a time. Say the adjective in brackets on the square and place it on your 'Master board'. Do *not* read out the adjective in BOLD TYPE as this is

what the students have on their boards. If the students have the opposite of the word you have called out, they cross it out.

4   Continue until a student has crossed out every word, in which case s/he shouts out *Bingo!*

5   Now you stop the game and ask the student to say the six adjectives on his/her card that s/he has crossed out. (You can ask another student to monitor this, to avoid any cheating!) Check on your board. They will be the words in **bold type** – the opposites of the words you called out.

6   If a mistake has been made, continue with the game until someone wins.

7   You can then play again with different cards. You might even ask one of the students to be the caller!

16 Matching pairs: Verb + noun collocations

Time: 25 minutes
Type of activity: Pairwork activity, based on matching the correct verb cards with the correct noun cards to form twenty common collocations.
Preparation: Copy and cut up the verb cards and the noun cards on pages 79–80 – one set for each pair/group, plus one set for yourself. To make it easier to distinguish between them, all the noun cards have a number 1–20.

Lexical area/Topic
Verb + noun collocations
answer the phone, ask a question, blow your nose, brush your teeth, build a house, climb a mountain, cook a meal, catch a cold, draw a picture, drink a cup of tea, drive a car, eat a biscuit, fasten a seatbelt, play the guitar, read a newspaper, ride a horse, sing a song, smoke a cigarette, switch on the television, write a letter

Method

1   Divide the class into pairs (or groups of three). Give each pair a set of verb cards and noun cards.

2   Tell them they have to arrange them into twenty pairs of words comprising a verb (on the left) and a noun (on the right). Tell them they can only use each word once, so if they think a verb or a noun can be used in two places, they have to choose one or the other.

3   Allow 15 minutes for this. Go round and check and help, if necessary.

4   Check orally with the whole class. Do it this way. Shuffle the noun cards and hold them up one at a time. Ask different pairs/groups to give you the corresponding verbs.

Key

answer – the phone (3); ask – a question (7); blow – your nose (13); brush – your teeth (20); build – a house (11); climb – a mountain (16); cook – a meal (17); catch – a cold (2); draw – a picture (1); drink – a cup of tea (6); drive – a car (9); eat – a biscuit (14); fasten – a seatbelt (15); play – the guitar (10); read – a newspaper (4); ride – a horse (19); sing – a song (18); smoke – a cigarette (5); switch on – the television (8); write – a letter (12)

17 Matching pairs: More mini dialogues

Time: 20 minutes
Type of activity: Pairwork activity, based on matching 2-line mini dialogues.
Preparation: Copy and cut up the opening words (A) and the replies (B) on pages 81–82 – one set for each pair/group, plus one set of A-cards for yourself.

Lexical area/Topic
Various useful phrases and responses
It's my birthday today. Many happy returns!
Would you like to come to my party? Yes, I'd love to.
I don't like opera. Neither do I.
This is my brother, Mark. Hello. Pleased to meet you. etc.

Method

1 Divide the class into pairs (or groups of three). Give each pair a set of A- and B-cards.

2 Tell them they have to arrange them into twelve mini dialogues, with the opening words (on the left) and the replies (on the right). Point out that the reply cards are numbered 1–12.

3 Allow 15 minutes for this. Go round and help, if necessary with vocabulary.

4 Check orally with the whole class. Do it this way. Shuffle the opening words (A-cards) and hold them up one at a time. Ask different pairs/groups to give you the corresponding reply.

Follow-up activity

1 Students work in pairs – A and B. One student (A) has all the A-cards, the other student (B) has the B-cards.

2 Student B places his/her face up in front of him/her.

3 Student A shuffles his/her and places them face down on the table. S/He takes up the top card and reads it out. Student B tries to reply with the correct response. If s/he does, the card is turned over. If not, Student A can guess the answer and 'claim' the card. If no one knows the answer, Student A places the card at the bottom of the pile, to be used later on.

4 Continue in this way until all the cards have been used up.

5 If time, the students change roles and do it again.

NOTE: To make it more difficult, see if Student B can answer *without* looking at the B-cards.

Key

It's my birthday today. (4); Would you like to come to my party? (8); I don't like opera. (11); This is my brother, Mark. (6); Have you met Sally? (2); Have you got a light, please?(12); (in a shop) Can I help you? (10); Do you mind if I smoke? (1); I hope it doesn't rain. (7); Help yourself to a sandwich. (9); Would you help me, please? (3); I can't come tonight, I'm afraid. (5)

18 Dominoes: Compound nouns 2

Time:	20 minutes
Type of activity:	Group activity, based on the game of dominoes, where the students have to make compound nouns and thus fit all the dominoes on the board. Be careful only to cut along the dashed lines. Do not cut the solid lines.
Preparation:	Copy the domino board on page 83 – one board per group. Also copy and cut up the dominoes on page 84 – again, one set per group.

Lexical area/Topic

Compound nouns

alarm clock, ashtray, basketball, bedroom, briefcase, butterfly, crossword, dustbin, earring, lifeguard, lipstick, motorway, necklace, nightdress, penknife, rainbow, timetable

Method

1 Divide the class into groups of 3–4. Give each group a board and a set of dominoes.

2 Point out that the board already contains one domino – namely *guard: butter.* Also point out that the drawings in the middle of the board are the nouns they have to find.

3 Tell them that they have to place the remainder of the dominoes on the board in such a way that the right-hand word of one domino goes with the left-hand word of another to form a completely new word. Do the first one with them *(washing machine)* to make sure they understand what they have to do.

4 Allow 15 minutes for this. Go round and help, if necessary with vocabulary.

5 Check by beginning with the first domino *guard: butter.* Continue in a clockwise direction until you end with *way: life.*

Key (dominoes)
The correct order (clockwise) is:

guard: butter; fly: ear; ring: pen; knife: basket;
ball: wheel; chair: lip; stick: rain; bow: ash; tray:
neck; lace: time; table: cross; word: bed; room:
night; dress: brief; case: dust; bin: motor; way: life

19 Half a crossword: Sports, hobbies and pastimes

Time:	30 minutes
Type of activity:	Group activity, based on a crossword. Each group has an incomplete crossword. By asking for and giving definitions, they try to fill in the missing words.
Preparation:	Copy the crosswords on page 85 (for Group A students) and on page 86 (for Group B students).

Lexical area/Topic
Sports, hobbies and pastimes
athletics, badminton, boxing, camping, chess,
dancing, darts, dressmaking, football, gardening,
golf, gymnastics, judo, knitting, pottery, rugby,
snooker, swimming, table tennis, yoga

Method

1 Before starting, if necessary revise the various sports, hobbies and pastimes.

2 It is also a good idea to revise ways of giving definitions. Write the following on the board:

It's a … (sport/hobby/pastime)
You use … (a ball/a racket/a tent, etc.)
You do it … (indoors/outdoors/alone/with other people)
You need … (to run fast/to sit still, etc.)
It's very … (exciting/violent/difficult/creative, etc.)
… (Name of famous person) is/was good at it.

Write up the word **basketball** on the board. Ask student to suggest a way of explaining what 'basketball' is. *(e.g. It's a sport. You do it indoors. You do it with others. You use a ball. You need to be tall. You try to throw the ball into a net. etc.)*

Then write up the word **painting**. Again ask for suggestions for how to describe the word 'painting'. *(e.g. It's a hobby or pastime. You can do it outdoors or indoors. It's very creative. You need to be good at drawing. Picasso was good at it. etc.)*

Keep the phrases on the board, so the students can have them for reference.

2 Divide the class into A and B groups of between 2–4 students per group. They sit facing each other. Give each group the appropriate crossword and allow them time to check through the words they will need to define before starting. If necessary, give individual help at this stage.

NOTE: On no account must they allow the other group to see their crossword.

3 Explain that they have to take it in turns to ask for a word that is missing from their crossword. They simply ask: *What's 3 down? What's 14 across?*, etc. The other group now try to give as clear a definition as possible to help them guess the word.

4 Set a definite time-limit (e.g. 25 mins.) and stop the students at the end of it, *whether they have finished or not*.

5 They can now compare crosswords and check any words they didn't fill in.

6 You can follow up by asking the groups to explain how they defined one or two words from the crossword.

20 Half a crossword: Useful verbs

Time:	30–35 minutes
Type of activity:	Group activity, based on a crossword. Each group has an incomplete crossword. By asking for and giving definitions, they try to fill in the missing words.
Preparation:	Copy the crosswords on page 87 (for Group A students) and on page 88 (for Group B students).

Lexical area/Topic
Useful verbs
cook, count, cry, dance, die, draw, dream, drink, drive, fly, forget, kiss, listen, lose, marry, phone, play, rain, read, run, sell, shoot, shut, sing, sleep, smell, smoke, swim, talk, teach, throw, wash, write

Method

1 Before starting, it is a good idea to revise ways of giving definitions for verbs. Write the following on the board:

It's a way of …
(walking/eating/speaking/moving) etc.

It means to … (drive past another car/laugh in a very loud way) etc.

It's another word for … (hit/look/talk) etc.

It's the opposite of … (arrive/sell/win) etc.

You do this … (when you are happy/in the bath/when you eat/in the day) etc.

Write up the word **sing** on the board. Ask student to suggest a way of explaining what 'sing' is. *(e.g. Pop singers and opera singers do it. Some people do it when they have a bath or shower.* etc.)

Then write up the word **sleep**. Again ask for suggestions for how to describe it. *(e.g. You do this at night. You can sometimes do it in the day if you are tired.* etc.)

Keep the phrases on the board, so the students can have them for reference.

2 Divide the class into A and B groups of between 2–4 students per group. They sit facing each other. Give each group the appropriate crossword and allow them time to check through the words they will need to define before starting. If necessary, give individual help at this stage.

NOTE: On no account must they allow the other group to see their crossword.

3 Explain that they have to take it in turns to ask for a word that is missing from their crossword. They simply ask: *What's 3 down? What's 14 across?*, etc. The other

group now try to give as clear a definition as possible to help them guess the word.

4 Set a definite time-limit (e.g. 30 mins.) and stop the students at the end of it, *whether they have finished or not.*

5 They can now compare crosswords and check any words they didn't fill in.

6 You can follow up by asking the groups to explain how they defined one or two words from the crossword.

21 Group the words 2: Nouns

Time: 20 minutes
Type of activity: Group activity, based on placing the correct nouns under the correct headings.
Preparation: Copy and cut up the cards on page 89 – one set per group.

Lexical area/Topic
Words groups (various nouns)
In the kitchen
cooker, fridge, frying pan, microwave
In the bathroom
shower, soap, toothbrush, towel
In the bedroom
bed, pillow, sheet, wardrobe
In the garden
bushes, flowers, lawn, shed

Method

1 Divide the class into groups of 4–5. Give each group a set of words. Do **not** hand out the headings yet!

2 Tell them they have to arrange the words into groups of four – where each word is linked in some way. (They will need a desk or table on which to work.)

3 Allow 10–12 minutes for this. Then give out the headings. Tell them that these are the headings the words should be arranged under. Allow 5 more minutes for them to complete the task.

4 Instead of just reading out the correct answers at the end, you might like to try the following:

Ask one group to tell you which words they have placed under *IN THE KITCHEN*. If they didn't get them all right, tell them which words are correct, e.g. *You got three right – cooker, fridge and microwave.* Move on to the next group and ask them if they can say what the missing word is. Continue in this way until all four words are given. (In the unlikely event that after going round the class you still haven't found four correct words, tell them the answer.)

Continue in this way with the remaining three groups. (By using this method of checking, it allows the groups to 'change their minds' and reshuffle their cards during the checking stage.)

Key

In the kitchen: *cooker, fridge, frying pan, microwave;* ***In the bathroom:*** *shower, soap, toothbrush, towel;* ***In the bedroom:*** *bed, pillow, sheet, wardrobe;* ***In the garden:*** *bushes, flowers, lawn, shed*

22 Complete the story

Time: 20 minutes
Type of activity: Teacher-led whole class activity with the students working in small groups of three. The teacher reads out a story with twenty gaps. As they listen, the students have to decide which word is missing in each gap.
Preparation: Copy the *Numbers 1–20* sheet on page 156 – one copy per group. Also copy and cut up the cards on page 90 – again, one set per group.

Lexical area/Topic
Various nouns, verbs, adjectives, adverbs, etc. missing from a popular fairy story
afraid, blue, breakfast, certain, disappointed, dripped, exactly, happily, journey, knocking, lightning, other, return, sensitive, spend, standing, unless, wife, wished, without

Method

1   Divide the class into groups of 3–4 per group. Give each group a copy of the *Numbers 1–20* sheet plus a set of cards. Tell the students to arrange the cards on the desk in front of them. Try to get them to arrange them into nouns, verbs, adjectives, etc. Allow 5 minutes for this. Go around and check that they understand the words.

2   Before reading out the story you may need to pre-teach some of the vocabulary. Do this with the whole class. If necessary, write the most difficult words up on the board.

3   Read out the story below. Say the number of the gap *as* you come to it. If necessary, read each sentence with a gap more than once. Make sure you clearly indicate (by making a sound, etc.) where each gap is.

4   The students look at their words and decide if they can find one which will fit into the gap in the part of the story you have just read out. They place it in box 1 for gap 1, box 2 for gap 2, and so on. Encourage them to guess, even if they aren't 100 per cent sure.

5   Continue in this manner until you have read out the complete story.

6   Check orally. Read the story again. Pause before each gap and ask for suggestions for the missing word. Give each group 1 point for each correct answer.

7   Which group scored the most?

Follow-up

The students shuffle their cards and place them face down on the table in front of them. They now spread them out like a pack of cards and pick out five at random. Working together, they try to write five gapped sentence for these cards.

Get them to read out their sentences. The rest of the class listen and try to guess what the missing words are.

STORY (to be read out by the teacher)

Don't forget to say the number of the gap *as* you come to it. And also to remind the students where to put their words. But try to read whole sentences each time, if possible, to keep the thread of the story going. (See gap 1 for example.)

The Princess and the Pea *by Hans Christian Andersen*

Say: This is gap 1. *Which word do you think is missing?* Once upon a time there was a prince who (1)___(bleep!)___ to marry a princess. *Choose your answer and put it in square 1.* (Continue in this way throughout.)

Only it had to be a real princess. He travelled all round the world to find one and, during his (2)___(bleep!)___, he found many. But there was always something wrong. He could not say (3)___(bleep!)___ what it was, but first one thing, then another didn't seem quite right. In the end, feeling tired and (4)___(bleep!)___, he returned to his palace, unhappy that he had not found a real princess to be his (5)___(bleep!)___.

One evening, a few days after his (6)___(bleep!)___, there was a terrible storm. The rain poured down and there was thunder and (7)___(bleep!)___. Suddenly, there was a loud (8)___(bleep!)___ on the palace door and the old king, the prince's father, went to open it. Who should be (9)___(bleep!)___ there but a beautiful princess, or at least she said she was a princess. But she looked terrible! Her hair was very wet and hung all over her face, while drops of water (10)___(bleep!)___ from her nose, and her clothes clung like rags to her body. But she said she was a real princess.

The king took her to see the queen.

'We'll soon see about that!' said the old queen to herself. (11)___(bleep!)___ saying a word, she went quietly to the spare bedroom. There, she took all the bedclothes off the bed, and put a little pea on the bottom of it. Then she laid twenty mattresses one upon the (12)___(bleep!)___ on top of the little pea. Next

she put twenty bedcovers upon the mattresses. This was the bed the princess was to sleep in.

Next morning, when the lovely princess came down to (13)___(bleep!)___, the king, queen and prince looked at her closely, for the queen had told the others what she had done.

'Excuse me, my dear,' said the old queen. 'How did you (14)___(bleep!)___ the night? I hope you slept well.'

'I'm (15)___(bleep!)___ not! I had an awful night. I hardly slept at all! I don't know what was in my bed, but it felt so hard and lumpy underneath me. I'm black and (16)___(bleep!)___ all over!'

The king, queen and prince started smiling (17)___(bleep!)___. It was clear that the lady was a real princess. For she had felt the little pea through twenty mattresses and twenty bedcovers. No one but a true princess could have such (18)___(bleep!)___ skin.

The prince was really happy and married her because at last he was (19)___(bleep!)___ that he had found a real princess. As for the little pea, it was put on a marble stand and exhibited in the Royal Museum. It is still there to this day, (20)___(bleep!)___ of course, it has been lost.

(Adapted from *Fairy Tales* retold by James Riordan, p. 107, Pyramid Books, 1988.)

Key

1 wished, 2 journey, 3 exactly, 4 disappointed, 5 wife, 6 return, 7 lightning, 8 knocking, 9 standing, 10 dripped, 11 Without, 12 other, 13 breakfast, 14 spend, 15 afraid, 16 blue, 17 happily, 18 sensitive, 19 certain, 20 unless

23 Word association maze

Time: 10 minutes
Type of activity: A simple maze-type activity based on associating pairs of words correctly in order to find a route through the maze.
Preparation: Copy the handout on page 91 – one copy per pair.

Lexical area/Topic
Various sets of paired nouns
bird and nest, book and library, car and motorway, cigarette and ashtray, cup and saucer, hair and comb, husband and wife, knife and fork, letter and envelope, school and pupils

Method

1   Divide the class into pairs and give each pair a copy of the handout.

2   Before starting, do some quick work on word association. Write the following words on the board:

vegetable   hand   keyboard   headline computer   newspaper   finger   onion

Ask the students to find four pairs of words which go together.
(Key: *vegetable – onion; hand – finger; keyboard – computer; headline – newspaper*)

3   Explain that the aim is to find their way through the maze, using ten pairs of words that 'go together'. Tell them that they can move from one square to another horizontally, vertically or diagonally. If necessary, draw the following on the board to demonstrate how you can move through the maze.

next move here	next move here	next move here
next move here	**PRESENT WORD**	next move here
next move here	next move here	next move here

4   Remind them that they must start in the top left-hand square with the word *car* and they must end in the bottom right-hand square with the word *library*. If you wish, do the first association with them – i.e. *car–motorway*. Make sure they understand that from motorway they could choose either of the following as the *next* word: briefcase *(vertical)* – dentist *(diagonal)* – letter *(horizontal)* – tree *(diagonal)*.

5   The students now work on their own. After 10 minutes, stop them. Check orally by

asking the pairs (at random) for each pair of words in order, from pair 1 to pair 10.

NOTE: To make it more difficult some 'false' pairs have been put in as distracters and prevent the students from getting through the maze in ten moves. They are: *train – station; dog – tail; bee – honey* and *shirt – tie*

Key

(Move–Word pair): *1 car – motorway; 2 letter – envelope; 3 cigarette – ashtray; 4 bird – nest; 5 school – pupils; 6 husband – wife; 7 hair – comb; 8 cup – saucer; 9 knife – fork; 10 book – library*

24 Vocabulary quiz: Food, shops and shopping

Time: 30 minutes
Type of activity: An activity for the whole class, working in teams. It is in the form of a vocabulary quiz based on food, shops and shopping.
Preparation: Copy the quiz sheet on pages 92–93 – one copy per team.

Lexical area/Topic
Various words to do with food, shops and shopping
a bar of chocolate, a bottle of milk, a box of matches, a packet of biscuits, a tin of soup, apple, bacon and eggs, baker, banana, bowl, Brazil, chilli con carne, bread, breakfast, butcher, cabbage, cakes, Can I have the bill, please?, carrot, cheap, chef, China, coffee, table, cooker, crisps, cucumber, cupboard, curry, customer, dessert, egg, expensive, fish, fish and chips, florist, fork, France, frying pan, furniture shop, grape, hammer, India, Italy, Japan, jeweller, leek, lemon, lettuce, lunch, main course, meat, Mexico, microwave, onion, orange, paella, Pakistan, pear, peas, pillow, plates, plum, post office, potato, ring, saucepan, servant, sofa, South Africa, spaghetti, Spain, spoon, stamp, starter, strawberry, sushi, Sweden, taste, toaster

Method

1   Divide the class into teams and give each team a copy of the quiz sheet.

2 Before starting, tell each group to appoint a team leader and to decide on a name for themselves. The team leader is responsible for doing all the writing. The teams now write their team name at the top of the quiz sheet.

3 The teams now try to complete the quiz. Tell them they only have 25 minutes in which to complete it. As they work, go around the class. Help with instructions, etc. but do not help with answers.

4 Stop everyone when time is up. Groups now exchange quiz sheets. Check orally with the whole class by reading through the questions again and asking the groups for the answers. Award points. (Total = 43). Tell the students to add up the scores and to hand back the quiz sheets. The team with the highest score is the winner.

5 Find out which team has won. Award them a prize, perhaps?

Key

*1 lunch 1 point; 2 cucumber (It's a vegetable.) 1 point; 3 red 1 point; 4 Drawing b 1 point; 5 carrot (It's orange.) 1 point; 6 1 –c; 2–d; 3–a; 4–e; 5–b 1 point for each correct answer (total 5 points); 7 (a) packet; (b) tin; (c) loaf; (d) box 1 point for each correct answer (total 4 points); 8 a toaster 1 point; 9 **Fruits** banana, lemon, orange, plum **Vegetables** leek, onion, peas, potato 1 point for each correct answer (total 8 points); 10 (a) Italy; (b) Japan; (c) India; (d) Spain; (e) Mexico 1 point for each correct answer (total 5 points); 11 a chef 1 point; 12 bill 1 point; 13 a fork 1 point; 14 flowers 1 point; 15 cheap 1 point; 16 These apples taste nice. (You always have an adjective after the verb 'to taste'.) 1 point; 17 Right 1 point; 18 (a) chips; (b) eggs 1 point for each correct answer (total 2 points); 19 main 1 point; 20 spoon, cooker, cupboard, plates, microwave; 1 point for each (total 5 points)*
TOTAL POSSIBLE: 43 POINTS

Pre-intermediate/ Intermediate

25 Find someone who ... 2

Time: 20 minutes
Type of activity: Ice-breaker activity for the whole class (working in groups of up to nine students).
Preparation: Copy and cut out the handouts on page 94–96 – one card for each student.

Lexical area/Topic
Various words
loo, nest, busker, beech, daffodil, etc.

Method

1 Demonstrate with the whole class first to make sure that everyone knows what they have to do. Write on the board the following card:

Find someone who ...
1 can name three unpleasant jobs. _____
2 can think of a synonym for 'wonderful'. _____
3 knows what is kept in a zoo. _____
4 can explain the phrase:
They blew up the bridge. _____

Demonstrate each question with a different student. Ask them what question they could ask if they wanted to know if another student could name three unpleasant jobs. *(Can you name three unpleasant jobs?)* Ask a student the question and write his/her answers on the board. Do the same with the other three questions.

2 Explain that they are now going to be given a card each with five questions on it.

3 Divide the class into two groups. Give each person in each group a card and allow time for the students to work out which questions to ask. (If there are fewer than eighteen in the class, make necessary adjustments. Similarly, if there are more

than eighteen, then some students will have to have the same card.)

4   The students now walk around the room (within their groups) trying to find answers to the five questions on their cards. To ensure that they talk to as many people as possible, tell them that they are only allowed to ask one question every time they talk to someone.(But they can ask that person again later on!)

5   They write down any answers to their questions, plus the name of the student who gave them the answer.

6   After a while (15 mins.), stop the activity, irrespective of whether everyone has found answers to all their questions.

7   As a quick follow-up, let each student read out one of the answers on his/her card. You might also take up any questions for which the students couldn't get answers.

Possible 'difficult' words

(The numbers in brackets refer to the various cards used.)

(1) loo = another word for 'toilet'; the drawing is of a caravan

(2) a nest is where a bird builds its home; the drawing is of a bowl; the opposite of profit is loss

(3) a busker is a street musician – someone who plays hoping that the public will give him/her money; the drawing is of a tap

(4) a beech is a type of tree; the drawing is of a torch

(5) a daffodil is a common British spring flower (it is yellow); the drawing is of a penknife

(6) a clutch is part of a car. (You press it with your foot when you change gear.); the drawing is of a lighthouse

(7) the drawing is of a mobile phone

(8) a heel is part of a shoe (or a foot); the drawing is of a ladder

(9) a leek is a vegetable with a long white stem and long flat green leaves. (It tastes a bit like an onion.); the drawing is of a tent; the American word for taxi is 'cab'

26 Bingo: Synonyms

Time: 10 minutes per game

Type of activity: Teacher-led bingo activity based on synonyms (adjectives), with the students working individually (or in pairs in larger classes).

Preparation: Copy the eight students' cards on pages 98–99 and cut them out – one card per student (or per pair if the class is large). If you plan to play the game twice, give each student two cards to start with. Also make one copy of the teacher's handout on page 97. (You will need to cut out the bottom half into small squares.)

Lexical area/Topic
Synonyms (various adjectives):
awful – terrible; correct – right; enormous – very big; expensive – dear; frightened – scared; good – looking – handsome; happy – glad; impolite – rude; mad – crazy; peculiar – strange; pleasant – nice; sad – unhappy; rich – wealthy; polite – well-mannered; quiet – silent; wonderful – marvellous

Method

1   If you think your students already know these synonyms, go on to 2. If not, before starting, choose random pairs and ask them for one of the words on their cards, e.g. *rude.* Ask anyone if they know what the opposite of *rude* is. *(impolite)* Continue like this with the other adjectives. Alternatively, you could write on the board all the words in brackets on your 'Master board'. Then go through them one by one, asking the students to say if they have a word on their card that means the same as the word on the board.

2   Give out the bingo cards. Allow the students a few minutes to look through

them before beginning. (If the class is large, students work in pairs.)

3 Put the sixteen squares you have cut up into some kind of container (hat, cup, etc.) and draw them out one at a time. Read out the adjective in brackets on the square and place it on your 'Master board'. Do *not* read out the adjective in bold type as this is what the students have on their boards. If the students have a word that means the same as the word you have called out, they cross it out.

4 Continue until a student has crossed out every word, in which case s/he shouts out *Bingo*!

5 Now you stop the game and ask the student to read out the six adjectives on his/her card that s/he has crossed out. (You can ask another student to monitor this, to avoid any cheating!) Check on your board. They will be the words in BOLD TYPE – synonyms of the words you called out.

6 If a mistake has been made, continue with the game until someone wins.

7 You can then play again with different cards. You might even ask one of the students to be the caller!

27 Matching pairs: British English and American English

Time: 30 minutes
Type of activity: Pairwork activity, based on matching British English and American English words.
Preparation: Copy and cut up the British English words and the American English words on pages 100–101 – one set for each pair/group, plus one set for yourself.

Lexical area/Topic
British English words and their American English equivalents
autumn – fall; bill (restaurant) – check; car park – parking lot; chemist (shop) – drugstore; chips – French fries; curtains – drapes; dustbin – garbage can/trashcan; film – movie; flat – apartment;
garden – yard; handbag – purse; holiday – vacation; lift – elevator; lorry – truck; pavement – sidewalk; petrol – gas; sweets – candy; taxi – cab; tin – can; trousers – pants

Method
1 Divide the class into pairs (or groups of three). Give each pair a set of British English and American English cards.

2 Tell them they have to arrange them into twenty pairs of words, with the British English word on the left and the American English equivalent on the right. (To help the students, the American English cards are numbered 1–20.)

3 Allow 15 minutes for this. Go round and check and help if necessary.

4 Check orally with the whole class. Do it this way. Shuffle the British English cards and hold them up one at a time. Ask different pairs/groups to give you the corresponding American English word.

Follow-up activity 1
1 Students work in pairs – A and B. Each pair has a set of cards. They shuffle them and place them face down on a pile in front of them.

2 Student A starts. S/He picks up the top card, says it then gives the British or American equivalent of the word. If correct, s/he keeps the card. If not, the card is placed at the bottom of the pile to be used later on.

3 It is now Student B's turn to pick up a card and to giver the British or American equivalent of it.

4 Play continues in this way until all the cards are used up. The students count their cards at the end. The person with the most is the winner.

Follow-up activity 2
1 Students work in pairs – A and B. Each pair has a set of cards. They shuffle them and place them face down on a pile in front of them.

2 Student A starts. S/He picks up the top card and decides if it's a British English or American English word. (e.g. s/he picks up the word *handbag*. Then s/he says *'This is a British English word. The American English word for it is 'purse'. What's the word?'*)

3 Student B guesses. If correct, s/he keeps the card. If not, Student A keeps the card. NOTE: If Student A picks up a card and doesn't know the British English or American English equivalent of the word, then s/he misses a turn and the card is placed at the bottom of the pack.

3 Student B now picks up a card and asks A for the British or American English equivalent.

4 Play continues in this way until all the cards are used up. The students count their cards at the end. The person with the most is the winner.

Key

autumn – fall (7); bill (restaurant) – check (11); car park – parking lot (16); chemist (shop) – drugstore (19); chips – French fries (4); curtains – drapes (10); dustbin – garbage can/trashcan (3); film – movie (8); flat – apartment (13); garden – yard (17); handbag – purse (1); holiday – vacation (12); lift – elevator (15); lorry – truck (2); pavement – sidewalk (5); petrol – gas (9); sweets – candy (20); taxi – cab (6); tin – can (18); trousers – pants (14)

28 Matching pairs: Where are they?

Time: 20 minutes
Type of activity: Pairwork activity, based on matching phrases with places or situations where you might hear them.
Preparation: Copy and cut up the phrases (A-cards) and the places/situations (B-cards) on pages 102–103 – one set for each pair, plus one set of the A-cards for yourself.

Lexical area/Topic
Various useful phrases and responses
A single to Brighton, please. (At a railway station.)
Are you being served? (In a shop.)
You may now kiss the bride! (At the end of a wedding ceremony.)
Could I have the bill, please? (At a restaurant.)
etc.

Method

1 Divide the class into pairs. Give each pair a set of A- and B-cards.

2 Tell them they have to arrange them into twenty matching pairs, with the phrases (on the left) and the places or situations where you might hear them (on the right). Point out that the places/situations cards are numbered 1–20.

3 Allow 15 minutes for this. Go round and help, if necessary with vocabulary.

4 Check orally with the whole class. Do it this way. Shuffle the phrases (A-cards) and hold them up one at a time. Ask different pairs/groups to give you the corresponding place or situation.

Follow-up activity

1 Students work in pairs – A and B. One student (A) has all the A-cards, the other student (B) has the B-cards.

2 Student B places his/her face up in front of him/her.

3 Student A shuffles his/her and places them face down on the table. S/He takes up the top card and reads it out. Student B tries to reply with the correct response. If s/he does, the card is turned over. If not, Student A can guess the answer and 'claim' the card. If no one knows the answer, Student A places the card at the bottom of the pile, to be used later on.

4 Continue in this way until all the cards have been used up.

5 If time, the students change roles and do it again.

NOTE: To make it more difficult, see if Student B can answer *without* looking at the B-cards.

Key

A single to Brighton, please (14); Are you being served? (4); You may now kiss the bride! (11); Any more fares, please? (17); Could I have the bill, please? (9); Anything to declare? (20); Keep the change! (15); Last orders, please! (1); This is your captain speaking. (7); A bottle of cough medicine, please. (16); Which floor do you want? (5); A wash and blow-dry, please. (19); Send him off, ref! (8); A first-class stamp, please. (12); Would the defendant please rise! (3); Say 'Cheese!' (18); Flight SK555 is now boarding through Gate 14. (10); Get on your marks ... get set, ... (6); Action! (13); Stop, thief! (2)

29 Dominoes: Compound nouns 3

Time:	20 minutes
Type of activity:	Group activity, based on the game of dominoes, where the students have to make compound nouns and thus fit all the dominoes on the board.
Preparation:	Copy the domino board on page 104 – one board per group. Also copy and cut up the dominoes on page 105 – again, one set per group. Be careful only to cut along the dashed lines. Do not cut the solid lines.

Lexical area/Topic
Compound nouns
bargain, contact lenses, courtroom, credit card, driving licence, estate agent, fingerprint, food poisoning, greenhouse, heart attack, ladybird, light bulb, mail order, mother tongue, seatbelt, traffic warden, youth hostel

Method

1   Divide the class into groups of 3–4. Give each group a board and a set of dominoes.

2   Point out that the board already contains one domino – namely *bulb: driving*. Also point out that the clues in the middle of the board are the nouns they have to find.

(They are *not* in the correct order round the board!)

3   Tell them that they have to place the remainder of the dominoes on the board in such a way that the right-hand word of one domino goes with the left-hand word of another to form a completely new word. Do the first one with them *(driving licence)* to make sure they understand what they have to do.

4   Allow 15 minutes for this. Go round and help, if necessary with vocabulary.

5   Check by beginning with the first domino *bulb: driving*. Continue in a clockwise direction until you end with *card: light*. As you check, write the words on the board to show that some words are joined together *(bargain, fingerprint)* while others remain as separate words *(contact lenses, driving licence)*. Tell the students they have to learn each new compound word as they come across it.

Key (dominoes)

The correct order (clockwise) is:

bulb: driving; licence: finger; print: green; house: mail; order: seat; belt: contact; lenses: heart; attack: youth; hostel: mother; tongue: food; poisoning: court; room: bar; gain: lady; bird: estate; agent: traffic; warden: credit; card: light

30 Half a crossword: Nouns

Time:	30 minutes
Type of activity:	Group activity, based on a crossword. Each group has an incomplete crossword. By asking for and giving definitions, they try to fill in the missing words.
Preparation:	Copy the crosswords on page 106 (for Group A students) and on page 107 (for Group B students). Also copy the *How to define words* sheet on page 157 – one per student.

Lexical area/Topic
Various nouns

advertisement, attic, avalanche, bar, bargain, beard, bucket, burglary, cage, cash, choir, comb, computer, cream, election, essay, eyelash, funeral, guitar, invention, nephew, niece, pet, plant, poem, snake, stream, suburb, suntan, thunder, view, wedding

Method

1   Before starting, give each person a copy of the *How to define words* sheet.

Go through the (Things/Objects/People) section briefly. Write a few words on the board and ask for suggestions as to how to define them, e.g.
a dictionary   a tyre   a traffic warden   an uncle   etc.
Tell the students to have this sheet handy during the activity.

2   Divide the class into A and B groups of between 2–4 students per group. They sit facing each other. Give each group the appropriate crossword and allow them time to check through the words they will need to define before starting. If necessary, give individual help at this stage.

NOTE: On no account must they allow the other group to see their crossword.

3   Explain that they have to take it in turns to ask for a word that is missing from their crossword. They simply ask: *What's 3 down? What's 14 across?*, etc. The other group now try to give as clear a definition as possible to help them guess the word.

4   Set a definite time-limit (e.g. 25 mins.) and stop the students at the end of it, *whether they have finished or not*.

5   They can now compare crosswords and check any words they didn't fill in.

6   You can follow up by asking the groups to explain how they defined one or two words from the crossword.

31 Sort out the clues: Types of people

Time: 30 minutes
Type of activity: Group activity, based on matching clues to the appropriate words in a completed crossword. All the words are types of people.
Preparation: Copy the crossword grid on page 108 – one copy per group. Also copy the clues sheet on page 109 – one copy per group.

Lexical area/Topic
Types of people
accomplice, acquaintance, ambassador, bachelor, celebrity, client, colleague, deserter, employee, employer, expatriate, genius, gossip, heir, hermit, hooligan, landlord, lodger, neighbour, opponent, orphan, partner, pedestrian, refugee, successor, tenant, tourist, traitor, twin, vegetarian, widow, witness

Method

1   Divide the class into groups of 4–5. Give each group a completed crossword plus a clue sheet.

2   Tell them they have to work out which clue goes with which word and to write the correct reference in the box in front of each clue: (*1 down, 15 across*), etc. Perhaps demonstrate one with the whole class, e.g. the word *employee (12 Across)*. Ask them to see if they can find the clue for this, namely *A person who is paid to work for someone else*. They now write *12 Across* in the space in front of this clue.

3   Set a definite time-limit (e.g. 25 mins.) and stop the students at the end of it, *whether they have finished or not*.

4   Check by asking the groups in turn, e.g. *What's the clue for 1 Across – OPPONENT?* etc.

5   A possible follow-up for the whole class would be to ask the students to turn over their crosswords, read out the definitions and see if they remember which words they refer to.

Key

The correct order (as laid out on the clues sheet, reading down) is:

10 Across, 9 Down, 24 Across, 15 Down, 23 Down, 1 Across, 30 Across, 27 Down, 25 Across, 17 Across, 29 Across, 2 Down, 22 Down, 4 Across, 11 Across, 26 Down, 10 Down, 16 Across, 19 Across, 3 Down, 18 Across, 8 Down, 20 Down, 6 Across, 29 Across, 14 Down, 13 Across, 5 Down, 21 Down, 9 Across, 7 Down, 12 Across

32 Word association dominoes 1

Time: 15–20 minutes per game
Type of activity: This is a freer, more open-ended variation of dominoes and is for groups of 3–4 students. (Alternatively, it can be played by three or four teams with two students per team.) The aim is to find links or associations between pairs of words.
Preparation: Copy and cut up the cards on pages 110–111 – one set per group.

Lexical area/Topic
Various nouns and adjectives
birds, birthday, book, cake, car, cat, cinema, clothes, doctor, family, fat, film, food, football, fruit, garden, ghost, happy, holiday, hospital, house, hungry, ill, jacket, job, library, milk, money, motorway, nervous, old, party, photograph, present, rain, restaurant, school, spider, summer, waiter

Method

1 Arrange the class into groups of 3–4. The students sit facing each other around a desk or table. Each group is given a set of cards.

2 It might be an idea the first time you try this activity to explain the rules by demonstrating with one of the groups. The rules are as follows:

• The cards are shuffled and each student is dealt eight, which s/he hides from the others. The remainder of the cards (the pack) are placed face down on the table.

• The top two cards from the pack are turned over and laid out on the table, e.g. *birds birthday*

• Decide who starts. Play will then continue in a clockwise direction. Player 1 looks at his/her cards and tries to find a word that can be linked to or associated with either the word *birds* or *birthday*. If s/he finds a link, s/he places the new word or words next to the one on the table, at the same time explaining orally the link. Let us suppose the student has the word *money*. S/He places it next to *birthday* and says, e.g. *I was given a lot of money on my birthday.* So now we have the following on the table: *birds birthday money*

• The rest of the group now decide whether to accept or reject the association. (In the case of a dispute, the teacher's word is final!) If accepted, the word *money* is placed on top of *birthday* so that there are always only two cards showing. So you now have on the table: *birds money*

• Play passes to the next player who now has to find associations for either *birds* or *money*. If the association is rejected, the student removes the word from the table and play passes on to the next person. Alternatively, if the player cannot make a link or association, s/he says *Pass*. The first person to get rid of all his/her cards wins.

• At any stage during the game a player may exchange one of his/her cards for a new one from the remaining cards in the pack. But this means forfeiting a turn!

3 Should the game go on too long, the teacher can say *Stop*, in which case the player with the least number of cards left is the winner.

Alternative game

A variation on the game would be to allow players to discard more than one word at a time if they can use several words from their hand to associate with one of the words on the table, e.g. for the above opening words *(birds, birthday)*, suppose a player had in his/her hand the following words: *money, book, garden, food, holiday, happy, spider, summer, sport*

s/he could say the following sentence and get rid of *three* cards instead of one:
*I got some **money** for my birthday and bought a **book** about **sport** with it.*
In this case, all three words are discarded, but the last one mentioned *(sport)* is the one that is now exposed.

33 The definition game

Time: 30 minutes
Type of activity: This is a teacher-led activity for the whole class which tests the students' ability to define words.
Preparation: Copy and cut up the cards on page 112. Shuffle them and place them face down on the desk in front of you. Also copy the *How to define words* sheet on page 157 – one per student.

Lexical area/Topic
Various nouns, verbs and adjectives
Nouns
brochure, dictator, divorce, election, profit, snake, witness
Verbs
arrest, complain, emigrate, exaggerate, hitchhike, rob
Adjectives
boring, exhausted, jealous, late, lazy, lonely

Method

1   Before starting, divide the class into four teams, A-D. Hand out the *How to define words* sheet and go through it with the class. If you wish, write a few random nouns, verbs and adjectives on the board, e.g. *picnic to crawl genius exciting timetable* etc.

Ask for suggestions as to how to define them.

2   Team A starts. One person from the team comes out to the front of the class. S/He picks up the top card and looks at the word. S/He now has 3 minutes only to give a definition of it so that his/her team can guess what the word is. (The teacher or another student can act as timekeeper and say *Start* and *Stop*.)

3   If the others in the team A guess the word, the team gets 1 point. (Only Team A is allowed to guess at this stage!)

4   If the student runs out of time, one of the other groups (in turn) is allowed to guess and thus gain an extra point. If A starts first, then it would be Group B to guess next, followed by Group C and finally Group D.

5   If none of the teams guess correctly, the teacher tells the class what the word is and invites the whole class to suggest possible definitions.

6   Continue in this manner until each team has had five turns at giving definitions (only fifteen of the cards will be used).

7   The team with the most points at the end wins.

34 The homophone game 1

Time: 20 minutes
Type of activity: This is a teacher-led activity for pairs or groups of three which tests the students' knowledge of homophones, i.e. words that sound the same yet are spelt differently and have different meanings.
Preparation: Copy and cut up the two handouts on page 113 – one for each pair/group.

Lexical area/Topic
Various homophones
meet – meat, our – hour, steal – steel, hear – here, stair – stare, dear – deer, their – there, sum – some,

flower – flour, right – write, take – tail, weather – whether, pair – pear, here – hear, wear – where, red – read, son – sun, week – weak, way – weigh, eight – ate

Method

1   Before starting, explain what homophones are, namely words that sound the same but have different meanings and spellings. Write the following examples on the board:

I	*eye*	*too*	*two*
sea	*see*	*it's*	*its*

2   Divide the class into pairs (or groups of three). Ask each pair to think up sentences using the above words. Check orally. Here are some possible sentences:
I live in Wales./He hit me in the *eye*.
I live in Wales *too*./Pamela has *two* brothers.
We live near the *sea*./Can you *see* that man over there?
It's Tuesday today, isn't it?/A cat usually licks *its* paw before it washes *its* face.

3   Now give out the first handout to each pair/group. Explain that you are going to read out twenty sentences. After you have read a sentence they must decide which of the two words you were using.

4   Read out the following. Pause after each one to allow the students time to choose their answers. Read each sentence twice if necessary.

1   Vegetarians never eat **meat**.

2   There was a sign outside the bar saying 'Happy **hour** between 5 and 7.'

3   When he was a child he used to sometimes **steal** from his mother's purse.

4   Am I speaking loudly enough? Can you all **hear** me?

5   Don't you know that it's rude to **stare** at people like that!

6   Are there many wild **deer** in your country?

7   Do you know where Paul and Sally live? I need **their** address and telephone number.

8   That **sum** is wrong. The answer should be 650, not 630.

9   To make bread you need some **flour**.

10 How often do you **write** letters?

11 Have you ever read the book *A Tale of Two Cities*?

12 I couldn't care less **whether** I get the job or not.

13 Would you like an apple or a **pear** for dessert?

14 I got this jacket in the Summer **Sale**.

15 My wife won't **wear** glasses. She prefers contact lenses.

16 He was a Manchester United fan and decided to paint his bedroom walls **red**.

17 Does the **sun** rise in the east or the west?

18 My uncle has always had a **weak** heart.

19 I daren't **weigh** myself. I know I've put on at least two kilos since June.

20 I'll see you outside the cinema at **eight**.

5   Check orally. Do this by reading out each sentence again and asking random pairs/groups to spell out which word was used.

Follow-up activity 1

Tell each pair/group to choose five pairs of words from their handout and to write their own sentences using one of the pair. When they have finished, they find another pair/group and take it in turns to read out their sentences and see if the other pair/group can guess which word was being used.

Follow-up activity 2

Still working in pairs or groups, hand out the second handout. This is a simple check exercise.
Allow five minutes then check orally.

Key (Sheet 2)

1 W (meet); 2 R; 3 R; 4 W (tail); 5 R; 6 W (week); 7 W (steel); 8 R; 9 W (their … there); 10 R

35 Opposites maze

Time: 10 minutes

Type of activity: A simple maze-type activity based on associating pairs of opposites (verbs) correctly in order to find a route through the maze.

Preparation: Copy the handout on page 114 – one copy per pair.

Lexical area/Topic
Opposites of verbs
to arrive – to leave, to ask – to answer, to laugh – to cry, to lend– to borrow, to live – to die, to love – to hate, to open – to close, to remember – to forget, to sink – to float, to sit down – to stand up, to stop – to start, to turn on – to turn off, to win – to lose

Method

1 Divide the class into pairs and give each pair a copy of the handout.

2 Explain that the aim is to find their way through the maze, using ten pairs of opposites. Tell them that they can move from one square to another horizontally, vertically or diagonally. *(See Activity 23, Word association maze on page 16.)*

3 Tell them that they must start in the top left-hand square with the verb *to stop* and they must end in the bottom right-hand square with the verb *to stand up*. If you wish, do the first pair with them – i.e. *to stop–to start*. Make sure they understand that from *to start* they could choose either of the following as the *next* word:
to teach *(vertical)* – to cry *(diagonal)* – to laugh *(horizontal)* – to bring *(diagonal)*.

5 The students now work on their own. After 10 minutes, stop them. Check orally by asking the pairs (at random) for each pair of opposites in order, from pair 1 to pair 10.

NOTE: To make it more difficult some 'false' pairs have been put in as distracters and prevent the students from getting through the maze in ten moves. They are: *to turn on – to turn off; to sink – to float; to work – to play* and *to live – to die.*

Key

(Move–Word pair): *1 to stop – to start; 2 to laugh – to cry; 3 to open – to close; 4 to lend – to borrow; 5 to ask – to answer; 6 to win – to lose; 7 to remember – to forget; 8 to love – to hate; 9 to arrive – to leave; 10 to sit down – **to stand up***

36 Board game: Categories 2

Time: 30 minutes

Type of activity: Board game for two teams, based on placing words correctly according to which category they belong to. There are ten categories altogether with four words per category.

Preparation: Copy the playing board on page 115 – one board per group (of two teams). Also copy the cards on page 116 – one set per group.

Lexical area/Topic
Various word groups
Insects
ant, beetle, mosquito, spider
Birds
cuckoo, eagle, owl, pigeon
Wild animals
bear, fox, lion, squirrel
Inside a house
attic, ceiling, hall, stairs
Fruit
cherry, grapes, melon, peach
Vegetables
cauliflower, cucumber, leek, lettuce
Jobs & occupations
caretaker, estate agent, solicitor, surgeon
Words to do with sleep and tiredness
drowsy, nightmare, nod off, snore
Transport/vehicles
barge, lorry, tram, van
Types of meat
beef, ham, pork, veal

Method

1 Divide the class into groups of four. Further divide each group into two teams – A and B. Give each team a copy of the board, plus a copy of the sheet of words.

2 If necessary, before they start, demonstrate with the whole class so they understand what they have to do. *(See Activity 10, Board game: Categories 1 on page 6.)*

3 Explain that they have to work out which four words go with the ten categories on the board. They take it in turns to choose a word from the word sheet, then to write the word under one of the categories, not forgetting to write A or B after the word so they know who wrote it at the end. At the same time both teams now cross out that word from the word sheet. Tell them that there should be four words under each category. Also tell them **not** to tell their opponents if they see that they have written the word under the wrong category because, at the end, they will score 1 point for each correct answer and deduct 1 point for each incorrect one! Also tell them that they can write more than four words under each heading, but that only four will be correct when they check! (This is to enable a team to put a word under the correct heading when their opponent has wrongly placed a word there.)

4 Allow approximately 25 minutes for this. Then stop everyone whether or not they have gone through all the cards.

5 Check orally with the whole class. Read out the headings and invite answers. Say which four words are correct and tell them that they score 1 point for each word they placed correctly and deduct 1 point for each word in the wrong place!

6 The teams add up their scores. Check which team – A or B won in each group. Also see who had the highest score in the class.

Possible 'difficult' words

mosquito = insect that can sucks blood and can cause malaria; *cuckoo* = bird that lays its eggs in another bird's nest; *caretaker* = person who looks after a building (janitor = AmE); *solicitor* = another word for lawyer; *drowsy* = sleepy; *nightmare* = a bad dream; *nod off* = to fall asleep; *barge* = flat-bottomed boat found often on canals; *veal* = meat from a calf

Key

Insects: *ant, beetle, mosquito, spider;* **Birds:** *cuckoo, eagle, owl, pigeon;* **Wild animals:** *bear, fox, lion, squirrel;* **Inside a house:** *attic, ceiling, hall, stairs;* **Fruit:** *cherry, grapes, melon, peach;* **Vegetables:** *cauliflower, cucumber, leek, lettuce;* **Jobs & occupations:** *caretaker, estate agent, solicitor, surgeon;* **Words to do with sleep and tiredness:** *drowsy, nightmare, nod off, snore;* **Transport/vehicles:** *barge, lorry, tram, van;* **Types of meat:** *beef, ham, pork, veal*

Intermediate/ Upper Intermediate

37 Word hunt

Time:	25 minutes
Type of activity:	Warm-up pairwork/group work activity
Preparation:	Copy the handout on page 117 – one copy for each pair/group.

Lexical area/Topic
Various words
attractive, container, dangerous, difficult, electricity, enjoy, expensive, feel, fragile, free time, frightened, happy, heavy, in the country, loud, nice, noise, nosebleed, on a diet, pocket, sharp, smell (n), taste (v), thin, unpleasant, vice versa, waist

Method

1 Divide the class into pairs or groups of three. Before starting, write the following example on the board:
Find at least two things that are very difficult to carry.

Ask for suggestions and write them on the board.

2   Now give each pair/group a copy of the handout. Allow 5 minutes for them to read through it. Explain any difficult vocabulary.

3   Let them work at their answers for 20 minutes. Then stop everyone whether they have finished or not.

4   Check orally, by asking different pairs/groups for their answers.

Key (2 suggested answers – others are possible)

1 A flight by Concorde, a Rolls-Royce car; 2 a pen, a pencil; 3 a rose, perfume; 4 a key, a business card; 5 smoking, bungee jumping; 6 winning the Lottery, passing an exam; 7 a nail, a stiletto knife blade; 8 a shirt, a jacket; 9 television, telephone; 10 the sun, a daffodil; 11 screeching of brakes, car alarm; 12 a piano, a wardrobe; 13 cream cakes, chocolates; 14 playing golf, walking; 15 mountains, farm animals; 16 a train, a cheetah; 17 a fridge, a TV set; 18 an egg, toilet paper; 19 a saucepan, a cooker; 20 sunglasses, a suitcase; 21 a bucket, a trunk; 22 rock it, pick it up; 23 a glass vase, chandeliers; 24 doing aerobics, running; 25 spiders, heights; 26 window, wine bottle; 27 beer, salmon; 28 a pretty face, nice figure (men about women); a good body, a nice smile (women about men); 29 a stamp, a bar of chocolate; 30 squeeze your nose, lie on your back

38 Puzzle it out

Time: 20–30 minutes
Type of activity: This is a problem-solving activity for groups of three to five students.
Preparation: Copy the handout on page 118 – one copy per group. Also copy the clues on page 119 – again one set per group.

Lexical area/Topic
Words to do with people – their jobs, characteristics, hobbies, interests, etc.
Jobs
estate agent, plumber, solicitor, surgeon, traffic warden

Characteristics
bossy, conceited, mean, optimistic, sociable
Interests/Hobbies
amateur dramatics, bird-watching, gardening, painting, tennis
Other words
widower, Australian, twin, bald, bilingual, look on the bright side, divorce, will (n), have green fingers, tradesman, dress rehearsal, binoculars, pass away, excellent, serve (n), wig, tip (v)

Method

1   Divide the class into groups or 3–5 students. Give each group a copy of the main handout, plus a set of clues.

2   Explain that there are five people staying at a hotel: Mr Petty, Mr Grove, Ms Williams, Ms Stevens and Mr Harvey. Using the clues, the students have to complete the missing information in the table, namely each person's job, character, interest or hobby, plus one other item of information.

3   Allow them about 5 minutes to read through the clues. If necessary, explain any words they don't understand.

4   Set a time-limit (e.g. 20 mins.) and stop everyone *whether they have finished or not.*

5   Check the answers orally.

Acknowledgement:
This is based on an idea from *Keep Talking* by Friederike Klippel, Cambridge University Press 1984, p.181.

Key

Room 101 – Mr Grove – traffic warden – sociable – gardening – is a twin

Room 102 – Ms Stevens – surgeon – optimistic – painting – is Australian

Room 103 – Mr Petty – plumber – conceited – amateur dramatics – is bald

Room 104 – Ms Williams – solicitor – mean – tennis – is bilingual

Room 105 – Mr Harvey – estate agent – bossy – bird-watching – is a widower

Teacher's notes

39 Matching pairs: Adjective + noun collocations

Time: 30 minutes
Type of activity: Pairwork activity, based on adjective plus noun collocations such as *a juicy orange, an urgent message*, etc.
Preparation: Copy and cut up the adjective cards and the nouns cards on pages 120–121 – one set for each pair. Also copy one set of the adjective cards for yourself.

Lexical area/Topic
Adjective + noun collocations
an abrupt ending, an active volcano, an ambiguous statement, a cool breeze, a deadly poison, a delicious meal, a fatal accident, a flat tyre, a golden opportunity, a haunted house, identical twins, an infectious disease, an ingenious plan, a juicy orange, a loyal friend, a lucky/narrow escape, a rough estimate/guess, a tricky problem, an urgent message, a vivid imagination

Method

1 Divide the class into pairs. Give each pair a set of adjective phrases (A-cards) and nouns (B-cards).

2 Tell them they have to arrange them into twenty 'normal' adjective + noun combinations, with the adjective cards on the left and the correct noun cards on the right. (To help the students, the noun cards are numbered 1–20.)
Demonstrate with the first sentence. Ask the students to find *A juicy* … Now ask them to find the noun that they think best completes the sentence. (Answer: *orange*.) Tell them that each card can only be matched up once.

3 Allow 15 minutes to match up the adjective–noun collocations. Go round and check and help if necessary.

4 Check orally with the whole class. Do it this way. Shuffle the adjective cards and hold them up and say them one at a time. Ask different pairs to give you the 'correct' noun.

Follow-up activity 1

1 Students work in pairs – A and B. Each pair has a set of cards. They shuffle the adjective cards and place them face down on a pile in front of them.

2 Student A starts. S/He picks up the top card, says it then suggests a suitable noun. If correct, s/he keeps the card. If not, the card is placed at the bottom of the pile to be used later on.

3 It is now Student B's turn to pick up a card and to suggest a noun to end it.

4 Play continues in this way until all the cards are used up. The students count their cards at the end. The person with the most is the winner.

5 The game can be repeated, but this time using the noun cards. One student picks up a card, says it, then suggests a suitable adjective to go with it.

Key

a juicy … orange (7); a haunted … house (19); an urgent … message (14); a vivid … imagination (16); a golden … opportunity (20); a flat … tyre (4); a cool … breeze (8) a loyal … friend (11); an ambiguous … statement (1); a fatal … accident (13); a delicious … meal (9); a tricky … problem (2); a close/narrow … escape (15); identical … twins (18); an abrupt … ending (3); a deadly … poison (10); an infectious … disease (5); an ingenious … plan/idea (17); an active … volcano (6); a rough … guess/estimate (12)

40 Dominoes: Compound nouns 4

Time: 30 minutes
Type of activity: Group activity, based on the game of dominoes, where the students have to make compound nouns and thus fit all the dominoes on the board.
Preparation: Copy the domino board on page 122 – one board per group. Also copy and cut up the dominoes on page 123 – again, one set per group. Be careful only to cut along

the dashed lines. Do not cut along the solid lines.

Lexical area/Topic
Compound nouns
beauty spot, bloodbath, bottleneck, brainwave, catwalk, couch potato, death penalty, facelift, figurehead, generation gap, honeymoon, human rights, junk food, manslaughter, soap opera, stag party, status symbol

Method

1   Divide the class into groups of 3–4. Give each group a board and a set of dominoes.

2   Point out that the board already contains one domino – namely *moon: stag*. Also point out that the clues in the middle of the board are the nouns they have to find. (They are in the correct order round the board!)

3   Tell them that they have to place the remainder of the dominoes on the board in such a way that the right-hand word of one domino goes with the left-hand word of another to form a completely new word. Do the first one with them *(stag party)* to make sure they understand what they have to do.

4   Allow 15 minutes for this. Go round and help, if necessary with vocabulary.

5   Check by beginning with the first domino *moon: stag*. Continue in a clockwise direction until you end with *penalty: honey*. As you check, write the words on the board to show that some words are joined together *(bottleneck, brainwave)* while others remain as separate words *(stag party, junk food)*. Tell the students they have to learn each new compound word as they come across it.

Key (dominoes)

The correct order (clockwise) is:

moon: stag; party: beauty; spot: junk; food: status, symbol: bottle; neck: soap; opera: face; lift: brain; wave: human; rights: figure; head: generation; gap: couch; potato: cat; walk: blood; bath: man; slaughter: death; penalty: honey

41 Carry on the story

Time: 15–20 minutes per game
Type of activity: Teacher-led activity based on trying to use random words to make up and continue a story.
Preparation: Copy and cut up the cards on pages 124–125. Place them into a hat (or similar container).

Lexical area/Topic
Various words
Nouns
accident, avalanche, burglary, cigarette, cinema, dinner party, drugs, motorbike, moustache, overcoat, ring, river, snake, sports car, station, the USA, toilet, toothache, traffic warden, wedding
Adjectives
big-headed, excited, frightened, generous, hungry, jealous, pregnant, stubborn, thirsty, wealthy
Verbs
hide, hijack, kiss, make a speech, run away
Others
Congratulations!, Good luck!, Help!, in love, I hate you!

Method

1   Divide the class into four groups, A-D. One person in each group will keep the score.

2   Pick out three cards (at random)* and write them on the board, e.g. *accident wedding river.*

3   Explain that the aim of the activity is to make up a story, working together as a class.

4   Group A begins. One person in the group starts the story. It can be about anything, but the person can't stop talking until s/he uses one or more of the words on the board. In order to know when the person has finished, s/he says *Pass* and the next group continues.

5   Every word used scores 1 point, so in any one turn a group can gain 1–3 points. Using the above words, the person might say, for example, *I was on my way to my cousin's **wedding** when the car I was in had*

*an **accident**. PASS!*
(2 points scored.)

6 Play now passes to Group B. Before they start, the teacher wipes out any words used, takes new ones from the pack and writes these on the board, e.g. *river cigarette I hate you!*.

NOTE: There should always be three words or phrases on the board at any one time.

7 Try to repeat the last sentence (or occasionally summarise the story) as you move from group to group, so the main idea of the story is kept alive.

8 The group with the highest number of points at the end wins.

NOTE: Try to make sure that a different person in the group speaks each time, although you can allow the group to confer, if the person seems to be having difficulty.

* Sometimes, if you're very unlucky, the three random words or phrases you choose at the start might make it difficult for a group to begin the story. You can, if you wish, deliberately choose three 'easy' words to start with – i.e. ones that are bound to generate a story.

Follow-up activity

Select ten words at random and write them on the board. The groups now have 5 minutes in which to construct a story, using as many of the words on the board as possible.
Each group reads out their story in turn.

42 Vocabulary quiz: People

Time: 30 minutes
Type of activity: An activity for the whole class, working in teams. It is in the form of a vocabulary quiz based on people.
Preparation: Copy the quiz sheet on pages 126–127 – one copy per team.

Lexical area/Topic
Various words to do with people
acquaintance, affectionate, bachelor, big-headed, board of directors, bossy, brave, bribe, brother-in-law, cast of actors, check-up, cheerful, colleague, cowardly, crew of sailors, cuddle, Customs officer, doctor, effective, efficient, elderly, employee, employer, excited, fiancée, generous, gossip (n), greedy, hermit, hooligan, hospital, hug, kiss, mean, mother-in-law, neighbour, nephew, niece, obstinate, older, orphan, overweight, panel of experts, pinch, pregnant, prejudiced (towards), prescription, punctual, refugee, reliable, skinny, spectator, staff of teachers, stare, stethoscope, strict, stubborn, survivor, team of football players, tickle, troupe of dancers, uncle, vain, victim, wade, widow, witty

Method

1 Divide the class into teams and give each team a copy of the quiz sheet.

2 Before starting, tell each group to appoint a team leader and to decide on a name for themselves. The team leader is responsible for doing all the writing. The teams now write their team name at the top of the quiz sheet.

3 The teams now try to complete the quiz. Tell them they only have 25 minutes in which to complete it. As they work, go around the class. Help with instructions, etc., but do not help with answers.

4 Stop everyone when time is up. Groups now exchange quiz sheets. Check orally with the whole class by reading through the questions again and asking the groups for the answers. Award points. (Total 38) Tell the students to add up the scores and to hand back the quiz sheets. The team with the highest score is the winner.

5 Find out which team has won. Award them a prize, perhaps?

Key

1 Drawing b. 1 point; 2 Wrong (He is my elder brother. (Elderly = old – elderly people.) 1 point; 3 an employee (The person who gives you a job is your employer.) 1 point 4 a gossip 1 point; 5 ***Positive:*** *affectionate, cheerful, generous, reliable;* ***Negative:*** *bossy, greedy, mean, vain 1 point for each (total 8 points); 6 She always arrives on time/early./She is always on time/early./She is never late. 1 point; 7 my nephew 1 point; 8 clever with words 1 point; 9 1 – d; 2 – c; 3 – a; 4 – e; 5 –*

b 1 point for each (total 5 points); 10 She is a very efficient secretary. 1 point; 11 a doctor (stethoscope = instrument a doctor uses to listen to a patient's heart and other sounds inside the body; prescription = a piece of paper on which a doctor writes an order for medicine) 1 point; 12 against 1 point; 13 orphan 1 point; 14 cowardly 1 point; 15 ·1 a bachelor, 2 a hermit, 3 a refugee, 4 a hooligan 1 point for each (total 4 points); 16 uncle (All the others are females.) 1 point; 17 a Customs officer/a Customs official 1 point; 18 pregnant 1 point; 19 obstinate 1 point; 20 hug, tickle, pinch, kiss, cuddle 1 point for each (total 5 points (wade = walk through water with effort)
TOTAL POSSIBLE: 38 POINTS

43 Half a crossword: Verbs

Time: 30 minutes

Type of activity: Group activity, based on a crossword. Each group has an incomplete crossword. By asking for and giving definitions, they try to fill in the missing words.

Preparation: Copy the crosswords on page 128 (for Group A students) and on page 129 (for Group B students). Also copy the *How to define words* sheet on page 157 – one per student.

Lexical area/Topic
Various verbs
abolish, admire, afford, annoy, boast, bribe, cure, dare, deny, discover, encourage, envy, estimate, exaggerate, execute, force, gossip, hesitate, invent, nag, obey, oversleep, overtake, play truant, pollute, quote, recognise, refuse, replace, satisfy, sneeze, survive, suspect, tow

Method

1   Before starting, give each person a copy of the *How to define words* sheet.

    Go through the section on verbs briefly. Write a few words on the board and ask for suggestions as to how to define them, e.g. *escape discourage stretch yawn* etc.

    Tell the students to have this sheet handy during the activity.

2   Divide the class into A and B groups of between 2–4 students per group. They sit facing each other. Give each group the appropriate crossword and allow them time to check through the words they will need to define before starting. If necessary, give individual help at this stage.

    NOTE: On no account must they allow the other group to see their crossword.

3   Explain that they have to take it in turns to ask for a word that is missing from their crossword. They simply ask: *What's 3 down? What's 14 across?*, etc. The other group now try to give as clear a definition as possible to help them guess the word.

4   Set a definite time-limit (e.g. 25 mins.) and stop the students at the end of it, *whether they have finished or not*.

5   They can now compare crosswords and check any words they didn't fill in.

6   You can follow up by asking the groups to explain how they defined one or two words from the crossword.

44 Half a crossword: Adjectives to describe people

Time: 30 minutes

Type of activity: Group activity, based on a crossword. Each group has an incomplete crossword. By asking for and giving definitions, they try to fill in the missing words.

Preparation: Copy the crosswords on page 130 (for Group A students) and on page 131 (for Group B students). Also copy the *How to define words* sheet on page 157 – one per student.

Lexical area/Topic
Various adjectives to describe people
affectionate, bossy, brave, cheerful, cruel, friendly, generous, handsome, honest, imaginative, irresponsible, jealous, lazy, mean, modest, moody, patient, polite, prejudiced, punctual, reliable, rude, selfish, sensible, sensitive, sociable, spoilt, stubborn, sympathetic, witty

Method

As Activity 43 above.

This time, before starting, go briefly through the adjectives section of the *How to define words* sheet and write a few adjectives on the board. Then get the class to try and define them, e.g. *slim optimistic shy clever* etc.

Tell the students to have this sheet handy during the activity.

45 Group the words: Verbs

Time: 20 minutes

Type of activity: Group activity, based on placing the correct verbs under the correct headings.

Preparation: Copy and cut up the cards on page 132 – one set per group.

Lexical area/Topic
Group the words (various verbs)
Ways of hitting
beat, flog, smack
Ways of laughing/smiling
chuckle, giggle, grin
Ways of stealing
burgle, rob, shoplift
Ways of crying
break down, sob, weep
Ways of walking
hike, march, stroll
Ways of speaking
chat, mumble, recite

Method

1 Divide the class into groups of 4–5. Give each group a set of words. Do **not** hand out the headings yet!

2 Tell them they have to arrange the words into groups of three – where each word is linked in some way. (They will need a desk or table on which to work.)

3 Allow 10–12 minutes for this. Then give out the headings. Tell them that these are the headings the words should be arranged under. Allow 5 more minutes for them to complete the task.

5 Instead of just reading out the correct answers at the end, you might like to try the following:

Ask one group to tell you which words they have placed under *WAYS OF HITTING*. If they didn't get them all right, tell them which words are correct, e.g. *You got two right – beat and smack.* Move on to the next group and ask them if they can say what the missing word is. Continue in this way until all four words are given. (In the unlikely event that after going round the class you still haven't found four correct words, tell them the answer.)

Continue in this way with the remaining three groups. (By using this method of checking, it allows the groups to 'change their minds' and reshuffle their cards during the checking stage.)

Key

Ways of hitting: *beat, flog, smack*
Ways of laughing/smiling: *chuckle, giggle, grin*
Ways of stealing: *burgle, rob, shoplift*
Ways of crying: *break down, sob, weep*
Ways of walking: *hike, march, stroll*
Ways of speaking: *chat, mumble, recite*

46 Phrasal verb maze

Time: 15 minutes

Type of activity: A maze-type activity based on finding the missing phrasal verbs in sentences in order to find a route through the maze.

Preparation: Copy the handouts on pages 133–134 – one for each pair.

Lexical area/Topic
Phrasal verbs
blow up, break up, bring out, call off, come into, get on, get over, give up, go out, go with, hold up, look into, look up, look up to, put off, put on, take after, try out, turn down, turn up

Method

1 Divide the class into pairs and give each pair a copy of the maze handout, plus a copy of the sentence sheet.

2 Explain that the aim is to find their way through the maze. They do this by finding out which phrasal verbs are missing in each of the twenty sentences. Tell them that they can move from one square to another horizontally, vertically or diagonally. (See teacher's notes for Activity 23 on page 16.) Also say that the phrasal verbs are in the correct order, i.e. the phrasal verb for sentence 1 is followed by the phrasal verb for sentence 2, and so on.

3 The first one has already been done, so remind them that they start in the top left-hand square with *turn up*. If you wish, do the next sentence with them too – i.e. *look into*. Make sure they understand that from *look into* they could choose either of the following as the *next* word:
take up *(vertical)* – look through *(diagonal)* – go off *(horizontal)* – blow up *(diagonal)*.

4 The student now work on their own. After 10 minutes, stop them. Check orally by asking the pairs (at random) for each phrasal verb in order, from sentence 1 to sentence 20.

Key

1 turn up; 2 look into; 3 blow up; 4 try out; 5 call off; 6 look up; 7 take after; 8 get over; 9 hold up; 10 come into; 11 look up to; 12 bring out; 13 give up; 14 break up; 15 get on; 16 go out; 17 go with; 18 put off; 19 turn down; 20 put on

47 The homophone game 2

Time: 30 minutes
Type of activity: This is a teacher-led activity for pairs or groups of three which tests the students' knowledge of homophones, i.e. words that sound the same yet are spelt differently and have different meanings.
Preparation: None

Lexical area/Topic
Homophones
piece – peace, mail – male, waist – waste, die – dye, scent – cent, bear – bare, fair – fare, board –
bored, plane – plain, feet – feat, story – storey, mist – missed, vain – vein, course – coarse, allowed – aloud

Method

1 Divide the class into pairs or groups of three. Before starting tell each pair/group to write the numbers 1–15 in a column on a separate piece of paper.

2 Read out the following words one at a time. After you have read out each word, allow the pairs/groups approximately 30–40 seconds to try to write down two possible words.
1 piece/peace; 2 mail/male; 3 waist/waste; 4 die/dye; 5 scent/cent; 6 bear/bare; 7 fair/fare; 8 board/bored; 9 plane/plain; 10 feet/feat; 11 story/storey; 12 mist/missed; 13 vain/vein; 14 course/coarse; 15 allowed/aloud

3 Continue in this manner until all 15 words have been read out.

4 Check orally. If you wish, get one person from each pair/group to write their answer on the board. Try to get them to explain the different meanings.

Key

1 piece – peace (a piece of paper/not war); 2 mail – male (letters/not female); 3 waist – waste (part of the body/to waste money); 4 die – dye (stop living/colour something); 5 scent – cent (perfume, smell/American coin); 6 bear – bare (wild animal/no clothes on); 7 fair – fare (just, light–haired/cost of travel); 8 board – bored (plank of wood/not interested); 9 plane – plain (aeroplane, tool/not fancy); 10 feet – feat (part of body/achievement); 11 story – storey (tale/floor of building); 12 mist – missed (type of fog/didn't hit); 13 vain – vein (proud, conceited/blood flows through it); 14 course – coarse (French course, golf course/rough, rude); 15 allowed – aloud (permitted/out loud, so it can be heard)

48 20-square: Explain the words

Time: 30 minutes

Type of activity: In this teacher-led activity, students have to try to explain the meaning of various words. The words are part of a phrase and are shown in italics.

Preparation: Copy the handout on page 135 – one per group. (If the group is large, make sure there are enough copies for every two to three students.) Also copy, cut up and shuffle the *Numbers 1–20* on page 156. Place the numbers face down in front of you.

Lexical area/Topic

Various adjectives, verbs and nouns

Adjectives

the average salary, a courageous soldier, to feel embarrassed, an exhausting day, a huge garden, a plump woman, a priceless painting, a temporary job

Verbs

to call off a meeting, to fall out with a friend, to limp along the street

Nouns

a successful barrister, a pleasant chat, a face full of freckles, a £1 million loss, a terrible pessimist, a £10,000 ransom, an ugly scar, the only survivor, a terrible earthquake

Method

1   Divide the class into four groups – A-D. Give each group sufficient copies of the handout. Decide which group will start (e.g. Group A). The game then continues in a clockwise direction.

2   Hold up the first number (e.g. 5). The first group look at square number 5 on the handout and try to explain the word in *italics*. In this case, they would have to explain 'a pleasant *chat*' *(e.g. a relaxed informal conversation with someone).*

3   If correct, everyone puts a cross through this square and writes in the letter of the group that gave the correct answer – in this case they would write *A* in the square.

4   If incorrect, the number is put at the bottom of the pack to be used later on in the game.

5   Play continues in this way. The team with the highest number of 'squares' at the end is the winner.

NOTE: The reason for using the number cards is that it creates a certain amount of suspense – no one knows which square is going to be next. This results in heightened attention.

Key (possible explanations)

1 huge = enormous, very big; 2 priceless = impossible to put a value on; 3 earthquake = natural disaster where the earth shakes, caused by the movements of the rock plates at the Earth's surface; 4 limp = walk with an uneven step, usually because of an injured leg; 5 chat = a relaxed informal conversation with someone; 6 temporary = not permanent; 7 ransom = money demanded for the release of someone who is being held prisoner; 8 average = here: the salary that most people have; 9 freckles = small light brown spots on the face, caused by the sun; 10 call off = cancel; 11 scar = a mark left on your skin by an old cut or wound; 12 pessimist = someone who always expects the worst to happen; 13 fall out = quarrel; 14 plump = slightly fat; slightly rounded and overweight; 15 exhausting = very tiring; 16 barrister = lawyer who works in the higher law courts; 17 courageous = brave; 18 embarrassed = feel self-conscious, ill at ease, uncomfortable, humiliated; 19 loss = no profit; when a company loses money; 20 survivor = someone who stays alive when others have died, e.g. in an accident

Upper Intermediate/ Advanced

49 Find someone who ... 3

Time:	20 minutes
Type of activity:	Ice-breaker activity for the whole class.
Preparation:	Copy the handout on page 136 – one copy for each student.

Lexical area/Topic
Various words

Method

1   Give each student a copy of the handout.

2   Give them time to read through the questions and ask you about anything they do not understand.

3   The students then stand up and walk around the room trying to find answers to the questions on their handout. To ensure that they talk to as many people as possible, tell them that they are only allowed to ask two questions every time they talk to someone.

4   They write down any answers to their questions, plus the name of the student who gave them the answer.

5   After a while (approximately 15 mins.), stop the activity and have a whole class feedback. Go through all the questions orally, asking random students to read out any answers they got for each one.

Key (suggestion only)

1 a tree (trunk = thick part of tree; bark = covering around the trunk; branch = grows out from trunk, 2 S/He tests people's eyes and sells glasses; 3 Choose two from: terrible, dreadful, horrible, appalling, etc.; 4 Under their shirts. (American people wear a vest over their shirt. In Britain this is called a waistcoat.); 5 Sleeping; getting to sleep; 6 curtains, wardrobe, petrol; 7 Choose five from: disagree, disappointed, district, distract, distance, disappear, etc.; 8 blunt, rude, invisible; 9 a drawing-pin (AmE thumbtack); 10 It means to tease someone.; 11 Choose two from: dislike,

loathe, can't stand, despise, abhor, etc.; 12 Choose five from: part, partner, parallel, particle, partridge, partial, participate, party, etc.; 13 A police officer. Handcuffs are a type of chain for holding a prisoner's wrists together.; 14 recipe = instructions for cooking; receipt = piece of paper you get when you buy something in a shop. It usually has the price, date, description of article on it.; 15 Choose two from: earthquake, typhoon, tidal wave, drought, famine, volcanic eruption, etc.; 16 Someone who arrives at a party without being invited to it.; 17 Choose three from: mouse, keyboard, Windows, program, hard disk, disk, disk drive, CD-Rom, file, back up, etc.; 18 b (a is a spider, c is a ladybird); 19 Choose three from: bee, tree, see, free, me, plea, tee, tea, flea, flee, agree, etc.; 20 An attic is a room at the top of a house – just below the roof.

50 Sort out the punch lines

Time:	15 minutes
Type of activity:	Reading activity where the students sort out the punch lines to twelve jokes.
Preparation:	Copy the handout on page 137 – one copy for each pair.

Lexical area/Topic
Various words

Method

1   Give each pair a copy of the handout.

2   Explain that the last line or 'punch line' of each joke is in the wrong place – they have got mixed up. Tell the students that they have to try and sort out which punch line goes with which joke.

3   Set a time-limit (e.g. 12 mins.) and stop them *whether they have finished or not.*

4   Check orally with the whole class. This can be done in dialogue form with the various student reading out loud in pairs, but this time putting in the 'correct' punch line.

(NOTE: a *rabbit hutch* is where you would keep a pet rabbit. It is usually made from wood and wire.)

Key

Joke 1 – (7), Joke 2 – (6), Joke 3 – (12), Joke 4 – (8), Joke 5 – (1), Joke 6 – (9), Joke 7 – (10), Joke 8 – (4), Joke 9 – (11), Joke 10 – (3), Joke 11 – (5), Joke 12 – (2)

(NOTE: Joke 1 – check something, check pattern; Joke 2 – catch a bus, catch a mouse in a trap; Joke 3 – a jersey is also something you wear; Joke 4 – lean (meat), also a verb 'to lean'; Joke 5 – flat battery (no power), flat shape; Joke 8 – keep hair in = not to fall out, also to keep something in a container; Joke 9 – to make hair wavy, wave with a flag; Joke 10 – 'coughing' sounds the same as coffin (for a dead body); Joke 11 – bath plug v electric plug; Joke 12 – put cream on the wasp, rather than the child)

51 Word association dominoes 2

Time: 15–20 minutes per game
Type of activity: This is a freer, more open-ended variation of dominoes and is for groups of three or four students. (Alternatively, it can be played by three or four teams with two students per team.) The aim is to find links or associations between pairs of words.
Preparation: Copy and cut up the cards page 138–139 – one set per group.

Lexical area/Topic
Various nouns, verbs and adjectives
advertise, ambitious, astrology, bald, bargain, boring, cheeky, conference, cruise, depressed, disappointed, drugs, earthquake, Eiffel Tower, elephant, envious, feel sorry for, fiancé(e), generation gap, get the sack, headline, housework, illegal, line-dancing, lonely, on strike, overweight, postpone, president, receipt, refugee, rubber plant, scared, shy, spaghetti, steal, surgeon, unemployed, weekend, wig

Method

1 Arrange the class into groups of three or four. The students sit facing each other around a desk or table. Each group is given a set of cards.

2 It might be an idea the first time you try this activity to explain the rules by demonstrating with one of the groups. The rules are as follows:

- The cards are shuffled and each student is dealt eight, which s/he hides from the others. The remainder of the cards (the pack) are placed face down on the table.

- The top two cards from the pack are turned over and laid out on the table, e.g. *surgeon wig*

- Decide who starts. Play will then continue in a clockwise direction. Player 1 looks at his/her cards and tries to find a word that can be linked to or associated with either the word *surgeon* or *wig*. If s/he finds a link, s/he places the new word or words next to the one on the table, at the same time explaining orally the link. Let us suppose the student has the word *bald*. S/He places it next to *wig* and says, e.g. *He was bald, so he used to wear a wig*. So now we have the following on the table: *surgeon wig bald*

- The rest of the group now decide whether to accept or reject the association. (In the case of a dispute, the teacher's word is final!) If accepted, the word *bald* is placed on top of *wig* so that there are always only two cards showing. So you now have on the table: *surgeon bald*

Play passes to the next player who now has to find associations for either *surgeon* or *bald* If the association is rejected, the student removes the word from the table and play passes on to the next person. Alternatively, if the player cannot make a link or association, s/he says *Pass*.

- The first person to get rid of all his/her cards wins.

- At any stage during the game a player may exchange one of his/her cards for a new one from the remaining cards in the pack. But this means forfeiting a turn!

3   Should the game go on too long, the teacher can say *Stop*, in which case the player with the least number of cards left is the winner.

NOTE: With verbs, the players are allowed to change the tenses!

Alternative game

A variation on the game would be to allow players to discard more than one word at a time if they can use several words from their hand to associate with one of the words on the table, e.g. for the above opening words (*surgeon, wig*), suppose a player had in his/her hand the following words: *drugs, refugee, shy, steal, weekend, envious, advertise, get the sack* – s/he could say the following sentence and get rid of *three* cards instead of one: *The surgeon thought he would **get the sack** when he was accused of **stealing drugs** from the hospital* In this case, all three words are discarded, but the last one mentioned (*drugs*) is the one that is now exposed.

52 Make two words

Time: 15 minutes
Type of activity: In this activity for pairs/groups the letters which form the end of one word also form the beginning of another word, e.g. fo–**od**–our.
Preparation: Copy the handout on page 140 – one for each pair/group. Fold the right-hand column containing the missing pairs of letters so that they can't be seen from the front.

Lexical area/Topic
Various words
blouse – secret, boat – attack, cabin – invent, camera – rain, centre – reason, clap – appear, cream – amount, eagle – leather, open – enemy, pilot – other, pretty – tyre, reach – choir, spoon – onion, toast – stream, woman – answer, yellow – owner

Method

1   Before starting, write the following on the board:

   SW_ _ AGE   RI_ _OICE

   Point to the first one *(SW_ _ AGE)* and ask the class if they can think of two letters which form the end of the first word and also form the beginning of the second one. *(Answer: IM … swim/image)*. Do the same with the second one. *(Answer: CH … rich/choice)*

2   Now divide the class into pairs (or groups of three). Give each pair/group a copy of the handout. Tell them not to turn back or look at the folded part of the handout yet!

3   Do the first one with the whole class, to make sure they understand what they have to do. (wom**an** – **an**swer)

4   Tell them they now have 5 minutes to fill in as many of the others as they can.

5   After 5 minutes, stop them and tell them to turn over the folded part of the handout. Explain that these are the missing pairs of letters.

6   Give them 5 more minutes to complete the task.

7   Check orally, by asking various pairs/groups for their answers.

NOTE: If they have come up with their own pairs of letters which fit, then allow these.

Key

1 woman – answer, 2 boat – attack, 3 cabin – invent, 4 blouse – secret, 5 centre – reason, 6 clap – appear, 7 yellow – owner, 8 eagle – leather, 9 pretty – tyre, 10 toast – stream, 11 cream – amount, 12 spoon – onion, 13 open – enemy, 14 pilot – other, 15 camera – rain, 16 reach – choir

53 Half a crossword: Crime, law and order

Time: 35 minutes
Type of activity: Group activity, based on a crossword. Each group has an incomplete crossword. By asking

for and giving definitions, they try to fill in the missing words.

Preparation: Copy the crosswords on page 141 (for Group A students) and on page 142 (for Group B students). Also copy the *How to define words* sheet on page 157 – one per student.

Lexical area/Topic

Various words to do with crime, law and order
accuse, arrest, arson, burglary, cell, court, crime, criminal, death penalty, defence, detective, fine, fingerprint, forgery, fraud, illegal, judge, jury, manslaughter, murder, perjury, police station, prison, prosecution, punishment, rape, rob, robbery, sentence, shoplifting, steal, theft, trial, verdict, violence, witness

Method

1 Before starting, give each person a copy of the *How to define words* sheet.

Go through the sections briefly. Write a few words on the board and ask for suggestions as to how to define them, e.g. *spy ransom kidnap truncheon* etc.

Tell the students to have this sheet handy during the activity.

2 Divide the class into A and B groups of between 2–4 students per group. They sit facing each other. Give each group the appropriate crossword and allow them time to check through the words they will need to define before starting. If necessary, give individual help at this stage.

NOTE: On no account must they allow the other group to see their crossword.

3 Explain that they have to take it in turns to ask for a word that is missing from their crossword. They simply ask: *What's 3 down? What's 14 across?* etc. The other group now try to give as clear a definition as possible to help them guess the word.

4 Set a definite time-limit (e.g. 30 mins.) and stop the students at the end of it, *whether they have finished or not.*

5 They can now compare crosswords and check any words they didn't fill in.

6 You can follow up by asking the groups to explain how they defined one or two words from the crossword.

Possible 'difficult' words

arson = deliberately setting fire to a building; *fine* = money you have to pay as a punishment for breaking the law; *forgery* = copying things such as banknotes, letters, official documents, etc. in order to deceive people; *perjury* = lying in court while giving evidence, when you have promised to tell the truth; *verdict* = official decision made by a jury in a court of law about whether a person is guilty or not guilty; *fraud* = getting money from someone by tricking or deceiving them; *manslaughter* = killing a person by accident or negligence; *prosecution* = opposite of defence; *rape* = forcing someone to have sex with you; *sentence* = a punishment that a judge gives to someone who has been found guilty of a crime; also a verb 'to sentence'.

54 Sort out the clues: Health words

Time: 30 minutes
Type of activity: Group activity, based on matching clues to the appropriate words in a completed crossword. All the words are to do with health.
Preparation: Copy the crossword grid on page 143 – one per group. Also copy the clue sheet on page 144 – one copy per group.

Lexical area/Topic

Health words
ache, allergic, bandage, bleed, blood pressure, bruise, contagious, crutches, cut, disease, faint, fracture, germs, hay fever, heart attack, illness, infectious, influenza, injury, measles, midwife, painful, painkiller, patient, prescription, scald, sedative, swollen, symptoms, unconscious, ward, wound, x-ray

Method

1   Divide the class into groups of 4–5. Give each group a completed crossword plus a clue sheet.

2   Tell them they have to work out which clue goes with which word and to write the correct reference in the space in front of each clue: (*1 down, 15 across*), etc. Perhaps demonstrate one with the whole class, e.g. the word *ward (13 Across)*. Ask them to see if they can find the clue for this, namely *A large room in a hospital where patients are looked after*. They now write *15 Across* in the space in front of this clue.

3   Set a definite time-limit (e.g. 25 mins.) and stop the students at the end of it, *whether they have finished or not*.

4   Check by asking the groups in turn, e.g. *What's the clue for 1 across – DISEASE?* etc.

5   A possible follow-up for the whole class would be to ask the students to turn over their crosswords, read out the definitions and see if they remember which words they refer to.

Key

Here is the correct order (reading from top to bottom on the clues sheet):

10 Down, 14 Across, 6 Down, 25 Across, 30 Across, 21 Down, 11 Across, 18 Down, 19 Across, 24 Across, 7 Down, 1 Across, 22 Down, 12 Across, 26 Across, 2 Down, 6 Across, 8 Down, 15 Across, 13 Down, 28 Across, 4 Down, 20 Across, 23 Down, 29 Across, 8 Across, 17 Down, 27 Across, 3 Down, 23 Across, 16 Across, 5 Down, 9 Across

55 Matching pairs: Parts of the body idioms

Time: 20 minutes
Type of activity: Pairwork activity, based on matching twenty idioms to do with the body with the correct definitions.
Preparation: Copy and cut up the idioms (A-cards) and the definitions (B-cards)

on pages 145–146 – one set for each pair/group, plus one set of B-cards for yourself.

Lexical area/Topic

Various parts of the body idioms
to be all fingers and thumbs, to catch someone's eye, to get cold feet, to give someone the cold shoulder, to have a chip on one's shoulder, to have green fingers, to make one's blood boil, to pay through the nose for something, to pull someone's leg, to put one's foot in it, to stick one's neck out, to stretch one's legs

Method

1   Divide the class into pairs. Give each pair a set of A- and B-cards.

2   Tell them they have to arrange them into two columns, with the idioms on the left and the definitions on the right. Point out that the definition cards are numbered 1–12.

3   Allow 15 minutes for this. Go round and help, if necessary with vocabulary.

4   Check orally with the whole class. Do it this way. Shuffle the definitions (B-cards) and hold them up one at a time. Ask different pairs to give you the corresponding idiom.

Follow-up activity 1

1   Students work in pairs, A and B. One student (A) has all the A-cards, the other student (B) has the B-cards.

2   Student B places his/her face up in front of him/her.

3   Student A shuffles his/her and places them face down on the table. S/He takes up the top card and reads it out. Student B tries to reply with the correct response. If s/he does, the card is turned over. If not, Student A can guess the answer and 'claim' the card. If no one knows the answer, Student A places the card at the bottom of the pile, to be used later on.

4   Continue in this way until all the cards have been used up.

5   If time, the students change roles and do it again.

NOTE: To make it more difficult, see if Student B can answer *without* looking at the B-cards.

Key to cards

to be all fingers and thumbs (3); to catch someone's eye (6); to get cold feet (11); to give someone the cold shoulder (5); to have a chip on your shoulder (1); to have green fingers (4); to make your blood boil (12); to pay through the nose for something (10); to pull someone's leg (7); to put your foot in it (2); to stick your neck out (9); to stretch your legs (8)

56 What does it mean?

Time: 20 minutes

Type of activity: This teacher-led activity tests the students' knowledge of idioms. They work in pairs or groups.

Preparation: Copy the handout on page 147 – one for each pair/group.

Lexical area/Topic
Various idioms
be a bit thin on top, be given the sack, be in a rut, be over the moon, be taken for a ride, be tickled pink, blow one's top, have butterflies in one's stomach, have the gift of the gab, lose one's head, My lips are sealed!, put one's foot in it, slip one's mind, smell a rat, tighten one's belt, You could have knocked me down with a feather!

Method

1   Divide the class into pairs (or groups of three). Give each pair/group a copy of the handout. Allow them a few minutes to read through it. Do not explain anything while they do this.

2   Read out the following sentences, one at a time. (Read each one twice, if necessary.) Allow a minute or so after each one for the students to write the number of the sentence in the box next to the appropriate idiom.

Write the number 1 next to the person who has promised to keep a secret.
(*i My lips are sealed.*)

Write the number 2 next to the person who is good at talking.
(*c I've got the gift of the gab.*)

Write the number 3 next to the person who was very amused at something.
(*l I was tickled pink.*)

Write the number 4 next to the person who was very surprised.
(*a You could have knocked me down with a feather!*)

Write the number 5 next to the person who is feeling nervous.
(*o I've got butterflies in my stomach.*)

Write the number 6 next to the person who is extremely happy and excited.
(*f I'm over the moon.*)

Write the number 7 next to the person who has lost his job.
(*m They've given me the sack!*)

Write the number 8 next to the person who panicked.
(*p I lost my head.*)

Write the number 9 next to the person who is going to economise, and not spend too much.
(*d I must tighten my belt.*)

Write the number 10 next to the person who doesn't have much hair or is becoming bald.
(*g I'm a bit thin on top.*)

Write the number 11 next to the person who is leading a boring way of life which is difficult to change. (*b I'm in a rut.*)

Write the number 12 next to the person who forgot to do something.
(*k It slipped my mind.*)

Write the number 13 next to the person who has been deceived or tricked by someone.
(*n I've been taken for a ride.*)

Write the number 14 next to the person who lost his or her temper.
(*j I blew my top.*)

Write the number 15 next to the person who has made an embarrassing mistake. (*e I've put my foot in it.*)

Write the number 16 next to the person who is suspicious about something. (*h I smell a rat.*)

7 Check orally, by reading out each sentence again (possibly in a different order) and asking various pairs/groups for their answers.

Key

a 'You could have knocked me down with a feather!' 4; b 'I'm in a rut.' 11; c 'I've got the gift of the gab.' 2; d 'I must tighten my belt.' 9; e 'I've put my foot in it.' 15; f 'I'm over the moon.' 6; g 'I'm a bit thin on top.' 10; h 'I smell a rat.' 16; i 'My lips are sealed.' 1; j 'I blew my top.' 14; k 'It slipped my mind.' 12; l 'I was tickled pink.' 3; m 'They've given me the sack!' 7; n 'I've been taken for a ride.' 13; o 'I've got butterflies in my stomach.' 5; p 'I lost my head.' 8

57 Board game: Three-in-a-row

Time: 30 minutes
Type of activity: This activity is really a vocabulary quiz game for two teams plus a question master/mistress. It can be useful as an end-of-term 'fun' activity.
Preparation: Copy the *Three-in-a-row* board on page 148 – one for each team. Also copy the question sheets on pages 149–150 – again, one for each question master/mistress.

Lexical area/Topic
Miscellaneous vocabulary (questions and answers) *affectionate, amazed, ant, as old as the hills, assassinate, astounded, etc.*

Method

1 Divide the class into groups of five. Within each group, the students now divide themselves into two teams (A and B) plus a question master/mistress. Each team gets a master board while the question master/mistress gets the question sheets.

S/He must not let any of the teams see the questions!

2 Demonstrate with one team so the class can see how to play the game. Do it like this:

- Decide who begins (e.g. team A).
- Team A look at the board and choose an empty square (e.g. square 30). The question master/mistress now reads out the first question for Square 30.
- If correct, they write their letter (in this case A) in the square. (B do likewise, so both teams have an identical copy of the playing board at all times.)
- If incorrect, the answer is read out. (This question can't be used again.)
- Play continues in this way. The aim is for one group to 'capture' three adjacent squares – either vertically, horizontally or diagonally.
- Should team B also try to answer a question in square 30 and get it wrong (thus using up both questions), then this square is declared 'void' and they write a large X in it to show it can't be used further in the game.
- The game ends either when (a) one team gets three-in-a-row, or (b) all the squares are filled up. In the latter case, the team who have captured most squares wins.

3 The students now play the game. If there is time, they can play a new game. It doesn't matter that they have already heard some of the questions. Hopefully, the ones they got wrong they will get right this time.

58 Board game: Verbs

Time: 30 minutes
Type of activity: Board game for two teams, based on placing verbs correctly according to which category they belong to. There are eight

Preparation: categories altogether with five words per category.

Copy the playing board on page 151 – one board per group (of two teams). Also copy the word sheet on page 152 – one sheet per group.

Lexical area/Topic
Word groups (verbs)
Verbs to do with looking
gaze, glance, peep, squint, stare
Verbs to do with walking/running
dash, jog, limp, stagger, stroll
Verbs to do with speaking/listening
eavesdrop, lisp, mumble, overhear, stammer
Verbs to do with holding/pulling
drag, grasp, hug, tow, tug
Verbs to do with facial expressions
frown, grin, leer, pout, smile
Verbs to do with sounds people/animals make
bark, bleat, hiccup, neigh, snore
Verbs to do with shining/burning
flicker, glow, scald, singe, twinkle
Verbs to do with violence/death
assassinate, beat up, mug, pass away, stab

Method

1 Divide the class into groups of four. Further divide each group into two teams – A and B. Give each team a copy of the board, plus a copy of the sheet of words.

2 If necessary, before they start, demonstrate with the whole class so they understand what they have to do. *(See 10 Board game: Categories 1 on page 6.)*

3 Explain that they have to work out which four words go with the ten categories on the board. They take it in turns to choose a word from the word sheet, then to write the word under one of the categories, not forgetting to write A or B after the word so they know who wrote it at the end. At the same time both teams now cross out that word from the word sheet. Tell them that there should be four words under each category. Also tell them **not** to tell their opponents if they see that they have

written the word under the wrong category because, at the end, they will score 1 point for each correct answer and deduct 1 point for each incorrect one! Also tell them that they can write more than four words under each heading, but that only four will be correct when they check! (This is to enable a team to put a word under the correct heading when their opponent has wrongly placed a word there.)

4 Allow approximately 25 minutes for this. Then stop everyone whether or not they have gone through all the cards.

5 Check orally with the whole class. Read out the headings and invite answers. Say which four words are correct and tell them that they score 1 point for each word they placed correctly and deduct 1 point for each word in the wrong place!

6 The teams add up their scores. Check which team – A or B won in each group. Also see who had the highest score in the class.

Possible 'difficult' words

peep = to look quickly at someone or something, especially secretly through a small space or opening, e.g. a keyhole; *stagger* = to walk very unsteadily, with your body moving from side to side and almost falling, especially because you are injured, very tired or drunk; *eavesdrop* = to listen secretly to a private conversation; *stammer* = to have difficulty speaking because you cannot stop yourself from repeating the sound at the beginning of some words, e.g. *D..d..do ... you w..w..want ... ;* *tow* = to pull another vehicle or boat by a rope or a chain so that it moves along behind; *frown* = to make a slightly angry or unhappy expression with your face in order to show someone that you disapprove; *neigh* = the sound a horse makes; *twinkle* = to shine in the dark e.g. a star; *scald* = to injure part of your body by accidentally pouring hot liquid on it; *assassinate* = to kill a famous or important person for political reasons

Key

Verbs to do with looking: *gaze, glance, peep, squint, stare;* ***Verbs to do with walking/running:*** *dash, jog, limp, stagger, stroll;* ***Verbs to do with speaking/listening:*** *eavesdrop, lisp, mumble, overhear, stammer;* ***Verbs to do with holding/pulling:*** *drag, grasp, hug, tow, tug;* ***Verbs to do with facial expressions:*** *frown, grin, leer, pout, smile;* ***Verbs to do with sounds people/animals make:*** *bark; bleat, hiccup, neigh, snore;* ***Verbs to do with shining/burning:*** *flicker, glow, scald, singe, twinkle;* ***Verbs to do with violence/death:*** *assassinate, beat up, mug, pass away, stab*

59 New words from old

Time: 20 minutes
Type of activity: In this activity, students make words by adding one word to another, either before or after it. The new words formed are either single nouns or two-word nouns, e.g. hand*bag*, kit*bag*, *bag*pipes, etc. Students work in pairs or small groups.
Preparation: Copy the handout on page 153 – one for each pair/group.

Lexical area/Topic
Adding nouns to other words (before or after) to form completely new words:
armband, armchair, firearm, armpit bookend, guide book, bookmark, scrapbook cardboard, birthday card, credit card, scorecard etc.

Method

1 Divide the class into pairs or small groups. Give each pair/group a copy of the handout.

2 Go through the example with the whole class, so they understand exactly what they have to do. If necessary, go through number 1 too.

3 Check orally. After each group of four words, ask the students if they can think of even more similar words.

Key

1 arm (armband, armchair, firearm, armpit); 2 book (bookend, guidebook, bookmark, scrapbook); 3 card (cardboard, birthday card, credit card, scorecard); 4 coat (coat hanger, overcoat, raincoat, waistcoat); 5 light (candlelight, floodlight, lighthouse. skylight); 6 paper (paper clip, newspaper, wallpaper, paperweight); 7 ship (battleship, friendship, spaceship, shipwreck); 8 water (waterfall, waterproof, salt water, water melon); 9 ball (basketball, eyeball, snowball, ballroom); 10 room (bathroom, room service, classroom, changing room); 11 chair (armchair, chairwoman, pushchair, wheelchair); 12 house (houseguest, household, boarding house, housewife); 13 post (postbox, postcard, goalpost, lamppost); 14 board (boardroom, cupboard, dashboard, keyboard); 15 line (headline, coastline, deadline, line-up); 16 table (tablecloth, coffee table, tablespoon, timetable); 17 boy (pageboy, cowboy, boyfriend, boyhood); 18 step (stepfather, footstep, stepladder, instep); 19 box (chatterbox, gearbox, box room, postbox); 20 pot (flowerpot, coffee pot, pothole, teapot)

60 Vocabulary quiz: Idioms

Time: 30 minutes
Type of activity: An activity for the whole class, working in teams. It is in the form of a vocabulary quiz based on idioms.
Preparation: Copy the quiz sheet on pages 154–155 – one copy per team.

Lexical area/Topic
Various idiomatic expressions
a bird in the hand is worth two in the bush, a rolling stone gathers no moss, a sight for sore eyes, as keen as mustard, at the eleventh hour, be a bit thin on top, be a piece of cake, be behind bars, be hard up, be hen-pecked, be hot under the collar, be in a rut, be in two minds about something, be off one's head, be wet behind the ears, crow's feet, dog-eared, every cloud has a silver lining, etc.

Teacher's notes

Method

1 Divide the class into teams and give each team a copy of the quiz sheet.

2 Before starting, tell each group to appoint a team leader and to decide on a name for themselves. The team leader is responsible for doing all the writing. The teams now write their team name at the top of the quiz sheet.

3 The teams now try to complete the quiz. Tell them they only have 25 minutes in which to complete it. As they work, go around the class. Help with instructions, etc. but do not help with answers.

4 Stop everyone when time is up. Groups now exchange quiz sheets. Check orally with the whole class by reading through the questions again and asking the groups for the answers. Award points. (Total 33) Tell the students to add up the scores and to hand back the quiz sheets. The team with the highest score is the winner.

5 Find out which team has won. Award them a prize, perhaps?

Key

*1 Right. (He's inexperienced.) 1 point; 2 dog-eared (The corners of the pages are bent through use.) 1 point; 3 gate-crasher 1 point; 4 crow's feet 1 point; 5 He has died. 1 point; 6 'I smell a rat.' 1 point; 7 thin 1 point; 8 **Madness/Insanity:** have a screw loose, off one's head; **Fear:** hair-raising, have kittens; **Anger:** hot under the collar, throw a wobbly 1 point for each (total 6 points); 9 nose (It means to pay a lot more than it is worth.) 1 point; 10 work/their jobs 1 point; 11 the gift of the gab (It means he/she is good at talking.) 1 point; 12 off the cuff 1 point; 13 Dutch 1 point; 14 in prison/in jail 1 point; 15 (a) stone (b) two (c) Practice (d) silver (e) fire 1 point for each correct answer (total 5 points); 16 mutton dressed as lamb 1 point; 17 mustard 1 point; 18 It was easy. 1 point; 19 a husband (It means he is nagged and bossed about all the time.) 1 point; 20 hard up (short of money), make ends meet (manage on the money you get), a skinflint (mean person who doesn't like spending money), in the red (owe money to the bank, in debt) a nest-egg (money put aside for future use) 1 point for each (total 5 points) TOTAL POSSIBLE: 33 POINTS*

Part 2:
Material for photocopying

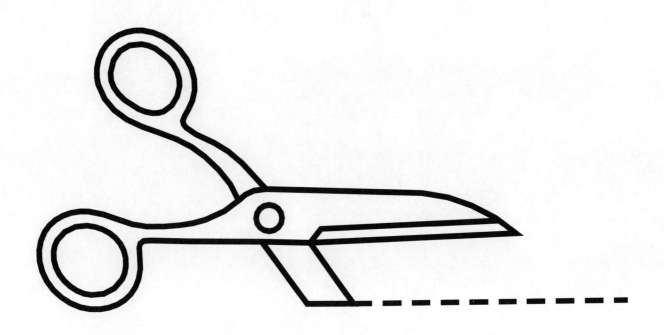

1 Find the words

Say: *Number … is a/an … and my name is …*   **Ask**: *How do you spell it?*

	It's a/an …	Student		It's a/an …	Student
1			2		
3			4		
5			6		
7			8		
9			10		
11			12		
13			14		
15			16		
17			18		
19			20		

1 Find the words

This is **a bag**.
Write it next to
drawing number 1.

When you meet
someone new, say:

Number 1 is a bag.

This is **a vase**.
Write it next to
drawing number 2.

When you meet
someone new, say:

Number 2 is a vase.

This is **a desk**.
Write it next to
drawing number 3.

When you meet
someone new, say:

Number 3 is a desk.

This is **an umbrella**.
Write it next to
drawing number 4.

When you meet
someone new, say:

*Number 4 is an
umbrella.*

This is **a chimney**.
Write it next to
drawing number 5.

When you meet
someone new, say:

*Number 5 is a
chimney.*

This is **a dentist**.
Write it next to
drawing number 6.

When you meet
someone new, say:

*Number 6 is a
dentist.*

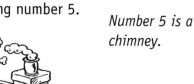

This is **a door**.
Write it next to
drawing number 7.

When you meet
someone new, say:

Number 7 is a door.

This is **a sausage**.
Write it next to
drawing number 8.

When you meet
someone new, say:

*Number 8 is a
sausage.*

This is **an ashtray**.
Write it next to
drawing number 9.

When you meet
someone new, say:

*Number 9 is a
ashtray.*

This is **a watch**.
Write it next to
drawing number 10.

When you meet
someone new, say:

*Number 10 is a
watch.*

Photocopiable

1 Find the words

This is **a chicken**. Write it next to drawing number 11.

When you meet someone new, say:

Number 11 is a chicken.

This is **a saucepan**. Write it next to drawing number 12.

When you meet someone new, say:

Number 12 is a saucepan.

This is **a spoon**. Write it next to drawing number 13.

When you meet someone new, say:

Number 13 is a spoon.

This is **a shop assistant**. Write it next to drawing number 14.

When you meet someone new, say:

Number 14 is a shop assistant.

This is a **biscuit**. Write it next to drawing number 15.

When you meet someone new, say:

Number 15 is a biscuit.

This is **a horse**. Write it next to drawing number 16.

When you meet someone new, say:

Number 16 is a horse.

This is **a carrot**. Write it next to drawing number 17.

When you meet someone new, say:

Number 17 is a carrot.

This is **a knife**. Write it next to drawing number 18.

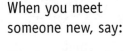

When you meet someone new, say:

Number 18 is a knife.

This is **an envelope**. Write it next to drawing number 19.

When you meet someone new, say:

Number 19 is an envelope.

This is **a pig**. Write it next to drawing number 20.

When you meet someone new, say:

Number 20 is a pig.

2 Bingo: Useful verbs

Teacher's master sheet

2 Bingo: Useful verbs

Teacher's cards

From *Vocabulary Games and Activities 1* by Peter Watcyn-Jones © Penguin Books 2001

2 Bingo: Useful verbs

Card 1

Card 2

Card 3

Card 4

2 Bingo: Useful verbs

Card 5

Card 6

Card 7

Card 8

 From *Vocabulary Games and Activities 1* by Peter Watcyn-Jones © Penguin Books 2001

3 Bingo: Things in the home

3 Bingo: Things in the home

Teacher's cards

3 Bingo: Things in the home

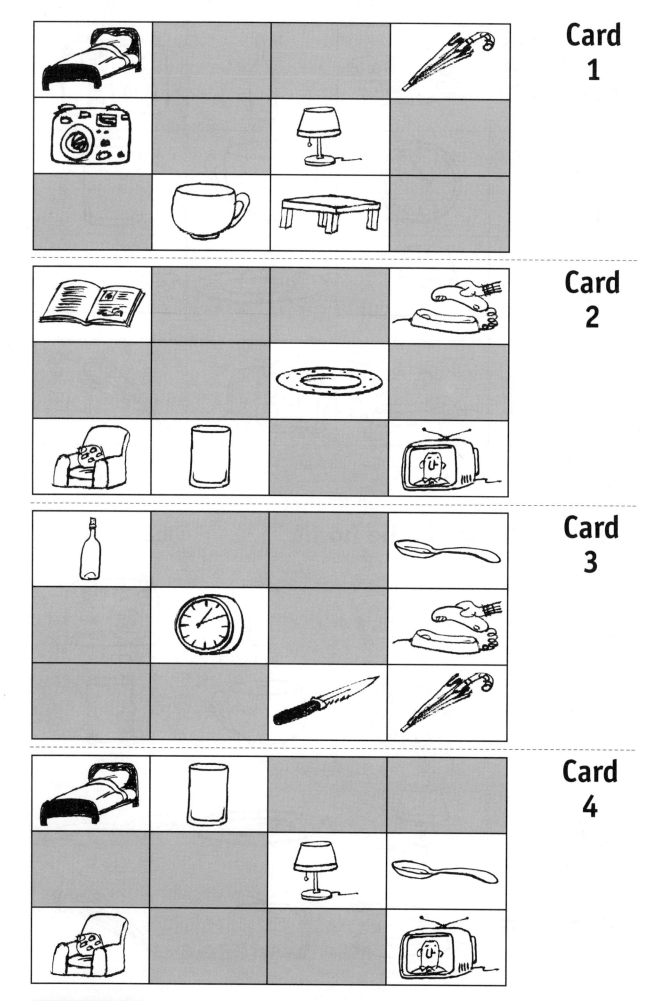

Card 1

Card 2

Card 3

Card 4

 From *Vocabulary Games and Activities 1* by Peter Watcyn-Jones © Penguin Books 2001

3 Bingo: Things in the home

Students' cards

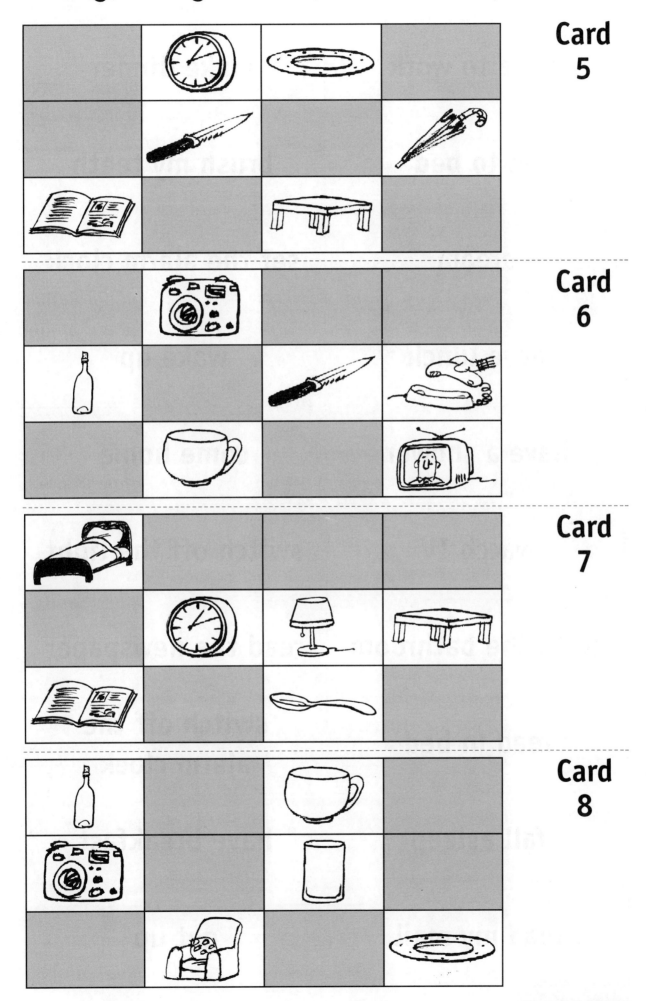

Card 5

Card 6

Card 7

Card 8

drive to work	make dinner
go to bed	brush my teeth
dream	set the alarm clock
have lunch	wake up
have a shower	come home
watch TV	switch off the light
go to the bathroom	read the newspaper
read in bed	switch off the alarm clock
fall asleep	have breakfast
read my mail	get up

 From *Vocabulary Games and Activities 1* by Peter Watcyn-Jones © Penguin Books 2001

4 Matching pairs: My day

From *Vocabulary Games and Activities 1* by Peter Watcyn-Jones © Penguin Books 2001

Hello. How are you?

What's your name?

How old are you?

I've just got married.

I'm sorry I'm late.

Where do you live?

Are you English?

Can you help me, please?

Would you like a cigarette?

What's the date today?

Have a nice weekend.

Thank you for helping me.

5 Matching pairs: Mini dialogues

1 *I'm nineteen.*

2 *No, I'm not. I'm Irish.*

3 *Thank you. The same to you.*

4 *In New York.*

5 *I'm fine, thanks.*

6 *No, thank you. I don't smoke.*

7 *Congratulations!*

8 *You're welcome!*

9 *That's all right.*

10 *Yes, of course.*

11 *It's Steve ... Steve Brown.*

12 *It's the tenth, I think.*

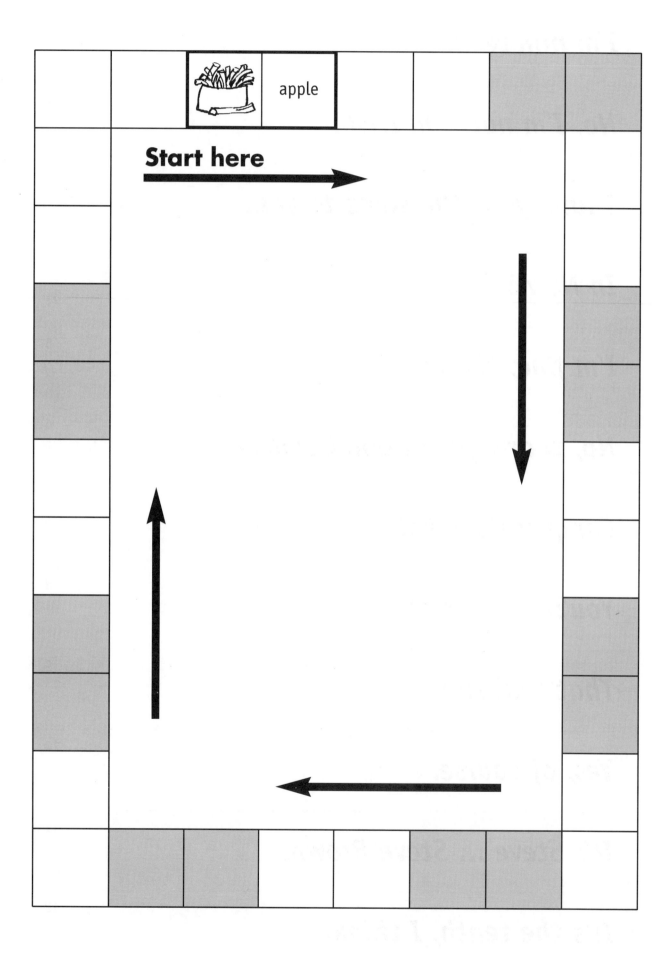

apple

Start here

From *Vocabulary Games and Activities 1* by Peter Watcyn-Jones © Penguin Books 2001

	ham-burger		cake		cheese		bread
	French fries (chips)		sandwich		pizza		chocolate
	rice		fish		banana		tomato
	ice-cream		meat		egg		orange

6 Dominoes: Food words

Dominoes

	ham-burger		cake		cheese		bread
	French fries (chips)		sandwich		pizza		chocolate
	rice		fish		banana		tomato
	ice-cream		meat		egg		orange

7 Dominoes: Compound nouns 1

Board

officer | washing

Start here

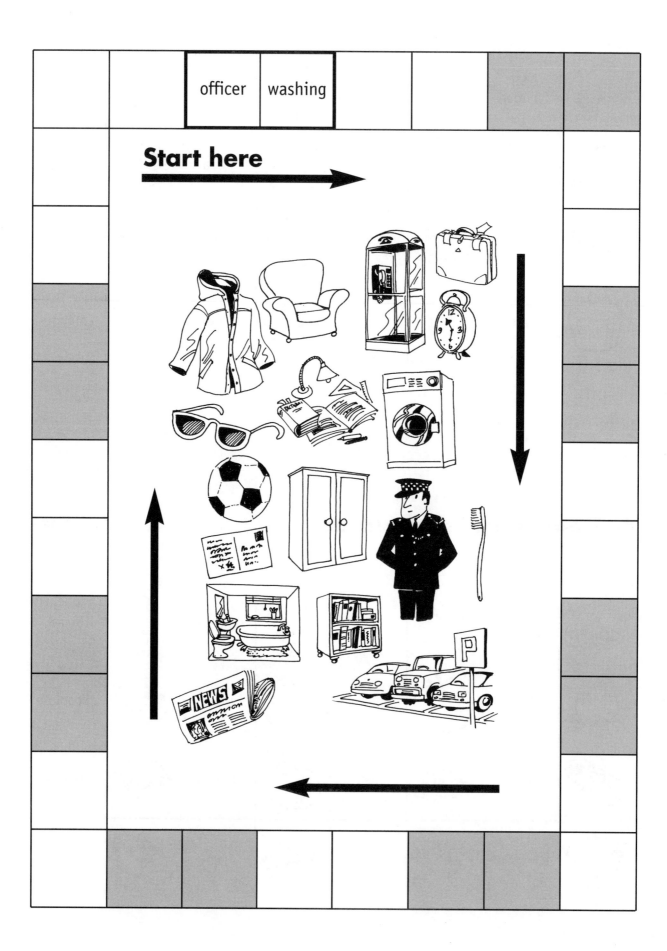

 From *Vocabulary Games and Activities 1* by Peter Watcyn-Jones © Penguin Books 2001

case	arm	glasses	tooth	park	home	case	alarm
paper	phone	ball	rain	machine	bath	board	police
chair	suit	room	car	clock	sun	box	post
brush	foot	card	cup	coat	news	work	book

7 Dominoes: Compound nouns 1

Dominoes

case	arm	glasses	tooth	park	home	case	alarm
paper	phone	ball	rain	machine	bath	board	police
chair	suit	room	car	clock	sun	box	post
brush	foot	card	cup	coat	news	work	book

8 Half a crossword: Jobs and people   Group A

Work in groups A and B. You are A.

Some of the words in the following crossword are missing. Group B know what they are. Group B also have some words that are missing from their crossword. They are the words at the bottom of the page.

Take it in turns to ask each other for a missing word. You can ask: **What's (1) Across? What's (6) Down?** etc.

Here are the words you will have to explain for Group B.

baby	doctor	hairdresser
boss	friend	nurse
brother	girl	teacher

    From *Vocabulary Games and Activities 1* by Peter Watcyn-Jones © Penguin Books 2001

8 Half a crossword: Jobs and people   Group B

Work in groups A and B. You are B.

Some of the words in the following crossword are missing. Group A know what they are. Group A also have some words that are missing from their crossword. They are the words at the bottom of the page.

Take it in turns to ask each other for a missing word. You can ask: **What's (1) Across? What's (6) Down?** etc.

Here are the words you will have to explain for Group A.

actor	husband	parents
bus driver	mother	student
dentist	neighbour	waiter

RELATIVES	BUILDINGS
TRANSPORT	**PARTS OF THE BODY**
department store	bicycle (bike)
finger	grandparents
bus	hospital
nose	aeroplane (plane)
uncle	hotel
mouth	aunt
car	ear
post office	cousin

10 Board game: Categories 1

Jobs	Furniture
Colours	**Fruit**
Vegetables	**Parts of the body**
'Action' verbs	**Things in a town**
Adjectives to describe people	**Things in the home**

10 Board game: Categories 1
Cards

dance	black	apple	bus stop
intelligent	bed	foot	dentist
carrot	lamp	beautiful	cinema
green	cucumber	chair	toe
street	clock	table	secretary
onion	friendly	swim	leg
bookcase	blue	radio	happy
bridge	yellow	climb	telephone
potato	banana	throw	back
pear	teacher	strawberry	shop assistant

 From Vocabulary Games and Activities 1 by Peter Watcyn-Jones © Penguin Books 2001

11 Pairwork cards: Clothes, etc.

Card 1

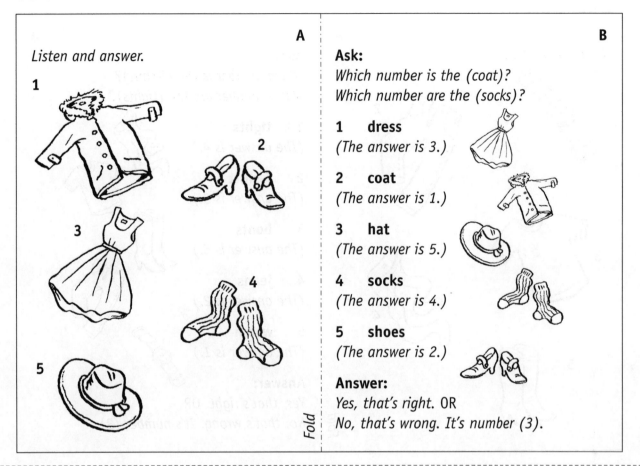

A

Listen and answer.

1

2

3

4

5

B

Ask:

Which number is the (coat)?
Which number are the (socks)?

1 **dress**
(The answer is 3.)

2 **coat**
(The answer is 1.)

3 **hat**
(The answer is 5.)

4 **socks**
(The answer is 4.)

5 **shoes**
(The answer is 2.)

Answer:
Yes, that's right. OR
No, that's wrong. It's number (3).

Fold

Card 2

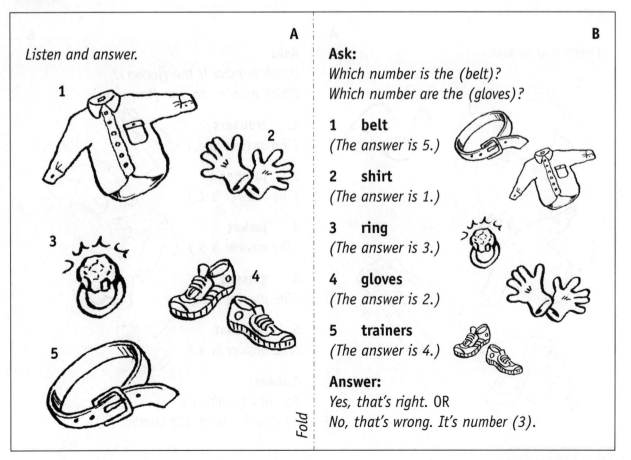

A

Listen and answer.

1

2

3

4

5

B

Ask:

Which number is the (belt)?
Which number are the (gloves)?

1 **belt**
(The answer is 5.)

2 **shirt**
(The answer is 1.)

3 **ring**
(The answer is 3.)

4 **gloves**
(The answer is 2.)

5 **trainers**
(The answer is 4.)

Answer:
Yes, that's right. OR
No, that's wrong. It's number (3).

Fold

From *Vocabulary Games and Activities 1* by Peter Watcyn-Jones © Penguin Books 2001   **Photocopiable**   71

11 Pairwork cards: Clothes, etc.

Card 3

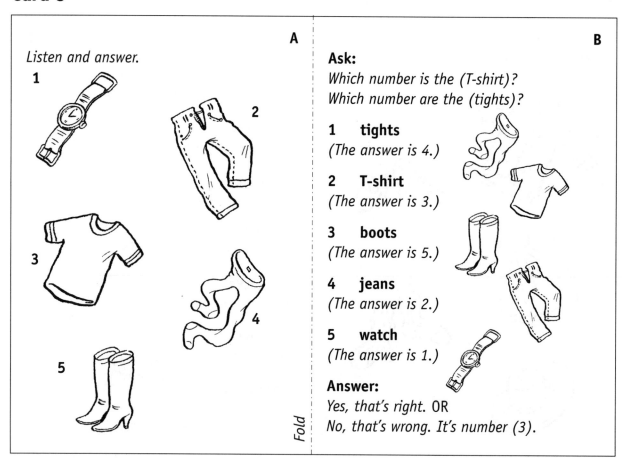

A

Listen and answer.

1
2
3
4
5

B

Ask:
Which number is the (T-shirt)?
Which number are the (tights)?

1   **tights**
(The answer is 4.)

2   **T-shirt**
(The answer is 3.)

3   **boots**
(The answer is 5.)

4   **jeans**
(The answer is 2.)

5   **watch**
(The answer is 1.)

Answer:
Yes, that's right. OR
No, that's wrong. It's number (3).

Fold

Card 4

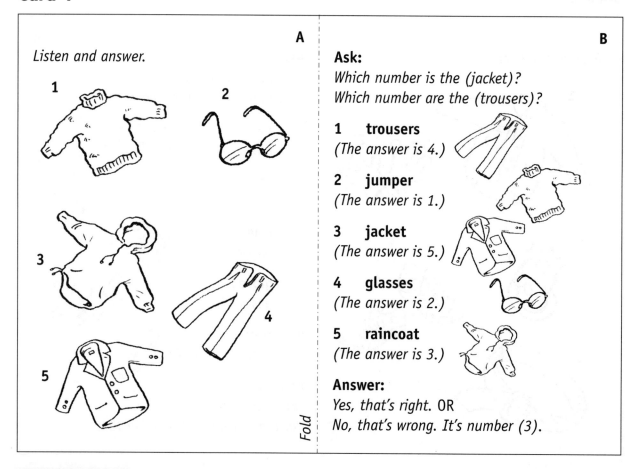

A

Listen and answer.

1
2
3
4
5

B

Ask:
Which number is the (jacket)?
Which number are the (trousers)?

1   **trousers**
(The answer is 4.)

2   **jumper**
(The answer is 1.)

3   **jacket**
(The answer is 5.)

4   **glasses**
(The answer is 2.)

5   **raincoat**
(The answer is 3.)

Answer:
Yes, that's right. OR
No, that's wrong. It's number (3).

Fold

     From Vocabulary Games and Activities 1 by Peter Watcyn-Jones © Penguin Books 2001

12 Complete the sentences

birthday	dirty	doctor	borrow
daughter	blonde	address	goldfish
invite	snow	spell	cheap
capital	department store	hungry	smile
foreigner	floor	ring	umbrella

From *Vocabulary Games and Activities 1* by Peter Watcyn-Jones © Penguin Books 2001

73

13 Find someone who ... 1

Find someone who knows the answers to the following.

1 Can you name two fruits?

2 Can you name two vegetables?

3 What is the opposite of
 rich? p_____
 big? s_____
 old? y_____

4 What you would buy at
 a baker?

 a butcher?

5 What is this creature called?

6 Can you name three of the colours
 of a **rainbow?**

7 Can you name two things found
 in the
 kitchen?

 bathroom?

 bedroom?

8 What do you usually keep in a
 wallet?

9 Can you name three **drinks?**

10 Can you name three things you can
 eat for lunch?

11 What is this called in English?

12 Can you name three **countries in
 Europe?**

13 Can you name three **animals** with
 four legs?

14 Can name two things worn by
 men?

 women?

15 Can you name this job?

 From Vocabulary Games and Activities 1 by Peter Watcyn-Jones © Penguin Books 2001

14 The alphabet race

Work in pairs. See how quickly you can work out the following.

A B C D E F G H I J K L M N O P Q R S T U V W X Y Z

1   What's the fourteenth letter of the alphabet?   _____

2   What's the seventh letter from the end of the alphabet?   _____

3   Make two words starting with the fourth letter of the
    alphabet.   _____

    _____

4   Make a 4-letter word using the first, twentieth, second
    and fifteenth letters of the alphabet.   _____

5   How many different letters are there in the word
    different?   _____

6   Make two words that end with the eighteenth letter of
    the alphabet.   _____

    _____

7   Which letters in the word *elephant* come between
    D and P in the alphabet?   _____

8   Which letter in the word *skirt* is furthest from N in the
    alphabet?   _____

9   Which letter comes twice in *camera* but only once
    in *mistake*?   _____

10 How many different vowels (V) and consonants (C) are   (V) _____
    there in the word *interesting*?
                                                           (C) _____

11 What is the position in the alphabet *(first, second, etc.)*
    of the middle letter in the word *chocolate*?   _____

12 Which letter is halfway between the fifth and fifteenth
    letters of the alphabet?   _____

13 Arrange the following words in alphabetical order:
    card comb carrot cream coffee

    _____   _____   _____   _____   _____

14 Which letter in the word *hair* is closest to N in the alphabet?   _____

15 Make a word that includes the third and sixteenth letters
    of the alphabet.   _____

15 Bingo: Opposites

BIG (small)	WEAK (strong)	DRY (wet)	FAST (slow)
CLEAN (dirty)	HAPPY (sad)	HARD (soft)	HOT (cold)
LIGHT (heavy)	GOOD (bad)	LOW (high)	OLD (young)
RICH (poor)	RIGHT (wrong)	TALL (short)	FAT (thin)

15 Bingo: Opposites

BIG (small)	WEAK (strong)	DRY (wet)	FAST (slow)
CLEAN (dirty)	HAPPY (sad)	HARD (soft)	HOT (cold)
LIGHT (heavy)	GOOD (bad)	LOW (high)	OLD (young)
RICH (poor)	RIGHT (wrong)	TALL (short)	FAT (thin)

Photocopiable   From *Vocabulary Games and Activities 1* by Peter Watcyn-Jones © Penguin Books 2001

15 Bingo: Opposites

Card 1

big			fat
fast		good	
	hard	rich	

Card 2

weak			right
		low	
clean	hot		tall

Card 3

dry			old
	happy		right
		light	fat

Card 4

big	hot		
		good	old
clean			tall

Card 5

	happy	low	
	light		fat
weak		rich	

Card 6

	fast		
dry		soft	right
	hard		tall

Card 7

big			
	happy	good	rich
weak		old	

Card 8

dry		hard	
fast		hot	
	clean		low

From *Vocabulary Games and Activities 1* by Peter Watcyn-Jones © Penguin Books 2001

answer	ask
blow	brush
build	climb
cook	catch
draw	drink
drive	eat
fasten	play
read	ride
sing	smoke
switch on	write

1 *a picture*	2 *a cold*
3 *the phone*	4 *a newspaper*
5 *a cigarette*	6 *a cup of tea*
7 *a question*	8 *the television*
9 *a car*	10 *the guitar*
11 *a house*	12 *a letter*
13 *your nose*	14 *a biscuit*
15 *a seatbelt*	16 *a mountain*
17 *a meal*	18 *a song*
19 *a horse*	20 *your teeth*

 From *Vocabulary Games and Activities 1* by Peter Watcyn-Jones © Penguin Books 2001

It's my birthday today.

Would you like to come to my party?

I don't like opera.

This is my brother, Mark.

Have you met Sally?

Have you got a light, please?

(in a shop) Can I help you?

Do you mind if I smoke?

I hope it doesn't rain.

Help yourself to a sandwich.

Would you help me, please?

I can't come tonight, I'm afraid.

No, of course not. 1

No, I don't think so. Hello. 2

Yes, certainly. 3

Many happy returns! 4

Oh, what a pity! 5

Hello. Pleased to meet you. 6

So do I. 7

Yes, I'd love to. 8

Thank you. 9

No, thank you. I'm just looking. 10

Neither do I. 11

I'm sorry, I don't smoke. 12

 From Vocabulary Games and Activities 1 by Peter Watcyn-Jones © Penguin Books 2001

18 Dominoes: Compound nouns 2 Board

| | | guard | butter | | | | |

Start here →

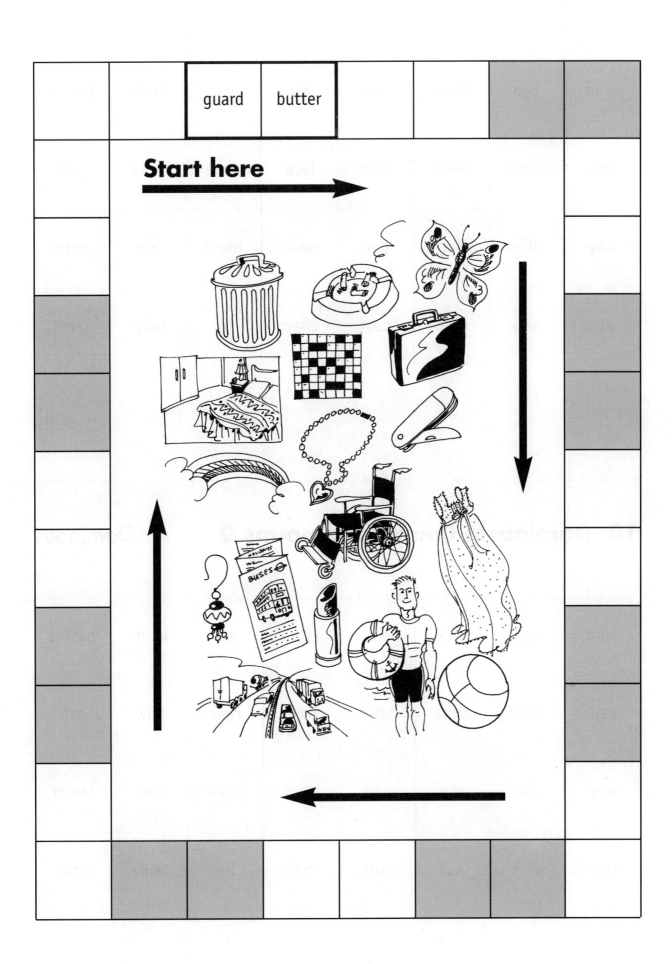

word	bed	stick	rain	fly	ear	knife	basket
ball	wheel	dress	brief	lace	time	bow	ash
way	life	ring	pen	room	night	bin	motor
tray	neck	case	dust	chair	lip	table	cross

18 Dominoes: Compound nouns 2 Dominoes

word	bed	stick	rain	fly	ear	knife	basket
ball	wheel	dress	brief	lace	time	bow	ash
way	life	ring	pen	room	night	bin	motor
tray	neck	case	dust	chair	lip	table	cross

19 Half a crossword: Sports, hobbies and pastimes

Work in groups A and B. You are A.

Some of the words in the following crossword are missing. Group B know what they are. Group B also have some words that are missing from their crossword. They are the words at the bottom of the page.

Take it in turns to ask each other for a missing word. You can ask: **What's (3) Across? What's (5) Down?** etc.

Here are the words you will have to explain for Group B.

athletics	dancing	gymnastics	knitting	rugby
chess	darts	judo	pottery	snooker

19 Half a crossword: Sports, hobbies and pastimes

Group B

Work in groups A and B. You are B.

Some of the words in the following crossword are missing. Group A know what they are. Group A also have some words that are missing from their crossword. They are the words at the bottom of the page.

Take it in turns to ask each other for a missing word. You can ask: **What's (8) Across? What's (1) Down?** etc.

Here are the words you will have to explain for Group A.

badminton	camping	football	golf	table tennis
boxing	dressmaking	gardening	swimming	yoga

 From Vocabulary Games and Activities 1 by Peter Watcyn-Jones © Penguin Books 2001

20 Half a crossword: Useful verbs   Group A

Work in groups A and B. You are A.

Some of the words in the following crossword are missing. Group B know what they are. Group B also have some words that are missing from their crossword. They are the words at the bottom of the page.

Take it in turns to ask each other for a missing word. You can ask: **What's (2) Across? What's (3) Down?** etc.

Here are the words you will have to explain for Group B.

cook	cry	dream	drink
forget	kiss	lose	play
rain	run	shut	sing
sleep	swim	teach	throw

20 Half a crossword: Useful verbs   Group B

Work in groups A and B. You are B.

Some of the words in the following crossword are missing. Group A know what they are. Group A also have some words that are missing from their crossword. They are the words at the bottom of the page.

Take it in turns to ask each other for a missing word. You can ask: **What's (6) Across? What's (1) Down?** etc.

Here are the words you will have to explain for Group A.

count	dance	die	draw
drive	fly	marry	phone
read	sell	shoot	smell
smoke	talk	walk	write

     From *Vocabulary Games and Activities 1* by Peter Watcyn-Jones © Penguin Books 2001

21 Group the words 2: Nouns

IN THE KITCHEN	IN THE BATHROOM
IN THE BEDROOM	**IN THE GARDEN**
fridge	wardrobe
towel	lawn
shed	cooker
bed	microwave
soap	flowers
shower	pillow
bushes	frying pan
sheet	toothbrush

other	breakfast	journey	wife
without	happily	wished	afraid
sensitive	return	unless	exactly
dripped	certain	standing	lightning
spend	blue	knocking	disappointed

From *Vocabulary Games and Activities 1* by Peter Watcyn-Jones © Penguin Books 2001

23 Word association maze

Work in pairs. See how quickly you can find your way through the maze. Start at the top with the word **CAR** and end at the bottom with the word **LIBRARY**. You should do it in ten moves only! (One pair of words = 1 move.)

START

car	tree	phone	roof	station
motorway	letter	envelope	family	train
briefcase	dentist	sky	cigarette	ashtray
wife	river	computer	house	bird
hair	husband	plate	umbrella	nest
comb	aeroplane	pupils	school	spider
cup	saucepan	shoe	gun	table
boat	saucer	knife	dog	tail
bee	park	fork	wine	tooth
honey	shirt	tie	book	library

FINISH

From *Vocabulary Games and Activities 1* by Peter Watcyn-Jones © Penguin Books 2001

24 Vocabulary quiz: Food, shops and shopping

Team name: _____   Quiz sheet

1   You eat **breakfast** in the morning. Which meal do you usually eat between 12–2 in the afternoon? _____

2   Which of the following is **not** a fruit?

grape ☐   cucumber ☐   pear ☐

3   What colour is a strawberry'? _____

4   Look at the following drawing.
Which one is the
frying pan – a, b or c?

a ☐   b ☐   c ☐

5   Which of these vegetables is **not** green? carrot ☐   cabbage ☐   lettuce ☐

6   Match up the following shops with what you can buy in them.

(1) baker (2) butcher (3) furniture shop (4) jeweller (5) post office

(a) a sofa (b) a stamp (c) bread and cakes (d) meat (e) a ring

Write your answers here:

1	2	3	4	5

7   We say a **bottle** of milk. What do we say for the following? (To help you, the first letter of the word is given.)

(a) A p _____ of biscuits.

(b) A t _____ of soup.

(c) A l _____ of bread.

(d) A b _____ of matches.

8   What's this?
(To help you, the letters
of the word are given,
but are mixed up.)

eastrot

Your answer: a _____

9   Place the following words next to the correct heading – (four words next to each)

banana, leek, lemon, onion, orange, peas, plum, potato

Fruits _____

Vegetables _____

From Vocabulary Games and Activities 1 by Peter Watcyn-Jones © Penguin Books 2001

10 Which countries do the following dishes comes from?
    Choose from the following:

    China, India, Sweden, Spain, South Africa, Italy, France, Brazil, Japan, Mexico

    (a) spaghetti _____   (b) sushi _____   (c) curry _____

    (d) paella _____   (e) chilli con carne _____

11 Which of the following people works in a restaurant?

    a chef ☐   a customer ☐   a servant ☐

12 What do you say when you want to pay at a restaurant?
    Could I have the _____, please?

    note ☐   cost ☐   bill ☐

13 Which of these would you **not** normally eat?

    fish ☐   an egg ☐   a fork ☐   crisps ☐

14 My cousin works in a **florist**.
    What does she sell? _____

15 The meal was **expensive**. What's the opposite of 'expensive'?
    (It starts with the letter 'c'.)

    c_____

16 Which of the following is correct?

    These apples taste nicely. ☐   These apples taste nice. ☐

17 Is this sentence right or wrong?
    I'd like a **bar** of chocolate, please.   Right ☐   Wrong ☐

18 Complete the following typical British dishes.

    (a) fish and c_____

    (b) bacon and e_____

19 At a restaurant, you normally have a starter, a _____ course and a dessert.

    chief ☐   main ☐   biggest ☐

20 Look at the eight words in the boxes. Choose five that are normally found in
    the kitchen.

spoon ☐	coffee table ☐	cooker ☐	pillow ☐
cupboard ☐	plates ☐	hammer ☐	microwave ☐

TOTAL SCORE: _____

25 Find someone who ... 2

Find someone who: 1

1 can name three things you would find in a **kitchen**. _____

2 can think of three words that start with **st-**. _____

3 knows what a **loo** is. _____

4 knows what this is.

_____

5 knows where you would find a **cushion**. _____

Find someone who: 2

1 can name three things you would find in a **bathroom**. _____

2 can think of three words that start with **ex-**. _____

3 knows which animal lives in a **nest**. _____

4 knows what this is.

_____

5 knows the opposite of the noun **profit**. _____

Find someone who: 3

1 can name three things you would find in a **bedroom**. _____

2 can think of three words that start with **cat-**. _____

3 knows what a **busker** is. _____

4 knows what this is.

_____

5 can think of three words that rhyme with **day**. _____

    From Vocabulary Games and Activities 1 by Peter Watcyn-Jones © Penguin Books 2001

25 Find someone who ... 2

Find someone who: 4

1 can name three things that are **sharp**.   _____

2 can think of three words that start with **sp**-.   _____

3 knows what a **beech** is.   _____

4 knows what this is.

_____

5 can think of three words that rhyme with **now**.   _____

- -

Find someone who: 5

1 can name three **wild animals**.   _____

2 can think of three words that start with **tr**-.   _____

3 knows what colour a **daffodil** is.   _____

4 knows what this is.

_____

5 can think of three words that rhyme with **clown**.   _____

- -

Find someone who: 6

1 can name three things that you can **drink**.   _____

2 can think of three words that start with **in**-.   _____

3 knows where you would find a **clutch**.   _____

4 knows what this is.

_____

5 can think of three words that rhyme with **spoon**.   _____

25 Find someone who ... 2

Cards

Find someone who:

7

1 can name three types of **meat**.

2 can think of three words that start with **re-**.

3 knows where you would find a **mattress**.

4 knows what this is.

5 can think of three words that rhyme with **hole**.

Find someone who:

8

1 can name three **buildings** found in a town.

2 can think of three words that start with **str-**.

3 knows where you would find a **heel**.

4 knows what this is.

5 can think of three words that rhyme with **love**.

Find someone who:

9

1 can name three **herbs** or **spices**.

2 can think of three words that start with **com-**.

3 knows what a **leek** is.

4 knows what this is.

5 knows the American word for **taxi**.

96 | Photocopiable | From *Vocabulary Games and Activities 1* by Peter Watcyn-Jones © Penguin Books 2001

26 Bingo: Synonyms

AWFUL (terrible)	CORRECT (right)	ENORMOUS (very big)	EXPENSIVE (dear)
FRIGHTENED (scared)	GOOD-LOOKING (handsome)	HAPPY (glad)	IMPOLITE (rude)
MAD (crazy)	PECULIAR (strange)	PLEASANT (nice)	SAD (unhappy)
RICH (wealthy)	POLITE (well-mannered)	QUIET (silent)	WONDERFUL (marvellous)

26 Bingo: Synonyms

Teacher's cards

AWFUL (terrible)	CORRECT (right)	ENORMOUS (very big)	EXPENSIVE (dear)
FRIGHTENED (scared)	GOOD-LOOKING (handsome)	HAPPY (glad)	IMPOLITE (rude)
MAD (crazy)	PECULIAR (strange)	PLEASANT (nice)	SAD (unhappy)
RICH (wealthy)	POLITE (well-mannered)	QUIET (silent)	WONDERFUL (marvellous)

From *Vocabulary Games and Activities 1* by Peter Watcyn-Jones © Penguin Books 2001

Photocopiable   97

26 Bingo: Synonyms

Card 1

awful			wonderful
expensive		peculiar	
	happy	rich	

Card 2

correct			polite
		pleasant	
frightened	impolite		quiet

Card 3

enormous			sad
	good-looking		polite
		mad	wonderful

Card 4

awful	impolite		
		peculiar	sad
frightened			quiet

    From *Vocabulary Games and Activities 1* by Peter Watcyn-Jones © Penguin Books 2001

26 Bingo: Synonyms

Card 5

	good-looking	pleasant	
	mad		wonderful
correct		rich	

Card 6

	expensive		
enormous		mad	polite
	happy		quiet

Card 7

awful			
	good-looking	peculiar	rich
correct		sad	

Card 8

enormous		happy	
expensive		impolite	
	frightened		pleasant

27 Matching pairs: British English words

autumn	bill (restaurant)
car park	chemist (shop)
chips	curtains
dustbin	film
flat	garden
handbag	holiday
lift	lorry
pavement	petrol
sweets	taxi
tin	trousers

 From Vocabulary Games and Activities 1 by Peter Watcyn-Jones © Penguin Books 2001

27 Matching pairs: American English words

1 *purse*	**2** *truck*
3 *garbage can/ trashcan*	**4** *French fries*
5 *sidewalk*	**6** *cab*
7 *fall*	**8** *movie*
9 *gas*	**10** *drapes*
11 *check*	**12** *vacation*
13 *apartment*	**14** *pants*
15 *elevator*	**16** *parking lot*
17 *yard*	**18** *can*
19 *drugstore*	**20** *candy*

28 Matching pairs: Where are they?

A single to Brighton, please.	Are you being served?
You may now kiss the bride!	Any more fares, please?
Could I have the bill, please?	Anything to declare?
Keep the change!	Last orders, please!
This is your captain speaking.	A bottle of cough medicine, please.
Which floor do you want?	A wash and blow-dry, please.
Send him off, ref!	A first-class stamp, please.
Would the defendant please rise.	Say 'Cheese!'
Flight SK515 is now boarding through Gate 14.	Get on your marks ... get set ...
Action!	Stop, thief!

 From Vocabulary Games and Activities 1 by Peter Watcyn-Jones © Penguin Books 2001

28 Matching pairs: Where are they?

1 In a pub (before it is about to close).	2 In the street (after being robbed).
3 In a courtroom.	4 In a shop.
5 Inside a lift.	6 At a racing track (before the start of a race).
7 On an aeroplane.	8 At a football match.
9 At a restaurant (just before you pay).	10 At an airport.
11 At a wedding (at the end of the ceremony).	12 At a post office.
13 On a film set.	14 At a railway station.
15 Inside/Outside a taxi (after paying).	16 At a chemist.
17 On a bus.	18 At a photographic studio (just before taking a photo).
19 At a hairdresser.	20 On passing through Customs.

| | | bulb | driving | | | | |

Start here

→

You need this to drive a car legally.

Burglars sometimes leave these on door handles, windows, etc.

A building made of glass for growing plants, etc.

Edison invented this.

You wear this in a car or a plane.

Plastic money?

An insect – red with black spots.

Your main language.

Ordering goods through the post.

This person buys and sells houses.

Worn instead of glasses.

You can die from this.

You might get this if you eat bad food.

Something bought at a good price.

A cheap place to stay.

The place where a trial is held.

This person checks cars – especially to see if they are parked wrongly.

←

From *Vocabulary Games and Activities 1* by Peter Watcyn-Jones © Penguin Books 2001

attack	youth	room	bar	print	green	warden	credit
hostel	mother	house	mail	bird	estate	lenses	heart
licence	finger	card	light	order	seat	poison-ing	court
gain	lady	agent	traffic	tongue	food	belt	contact

29 Dominoes: Compound nouns 3   Dominoes

attack	youth	room	bar	print	green	warden	credit
hostel	mother	house	mail	bird	estate	lenses	heart
licence	finger	card	light	order	seat	poison-ing	court
gain	lady	agent	traffic	tongue	food	belt	contact

30 Half a crossword: Nouns

Group A

Work in groups A and B. You are A.

Some of the words in the following crossword are missing. Group B know what they are. Group B also have some words that are missing from their crossword. They are the words at the bottom of the page.

Take it in turns to ask each other for a missing word. You can ask: **What's (9) Across? What's (3) Down?** etc.

Here are the words you will have to explain for Group B.

avalanche	choir	niece	stream
beard	comb	pet	suburb
burglary	cream	plant	view
cash	essay	snake	wedding

 From Vocabulary Games and Activities 1 by Peter Watcyn-Jones © Penguin Books 2001

30 Half a crossword: Nouns

Work in groups A and B. You are B.

Some of the words in the following crossword are missing. Group A know what they are. Group A also have some words that are missing from their crossword. They are the words at the bottom of the page.

Take it in turns to ask each other for a missing word. You can ask: **What's (1) Across? What's (6) Down?** etc.

Here are the words you will have to explain for Group A.

advertisement	bucket	eyelash	nephew
attic	cage	funeral	poem
bar	computer	guitar	suntan
bargain	election	invention	thunder

31 Sort out the clues: Types of people

In this crossword, all the words have been filled in. Sort out which clue goes with each word. Write the correct answer (1 Down, 8 Across, etc.) in front of each clue. Then arrange them in two columns with the Across clues on the left and the Down clues on the right.

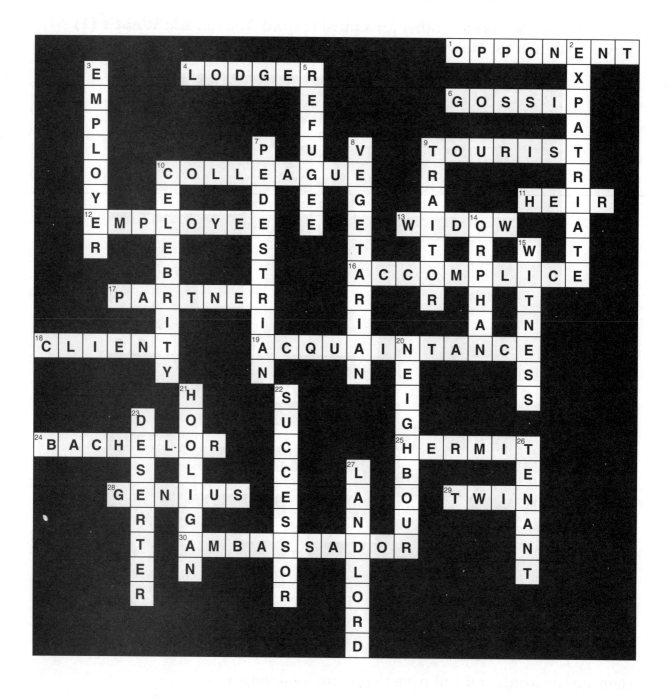

From *Vocabulary Games and Activities 1* by Peter Watcyn-Jones © Penguin Books 2001

31 Sort out the clues: Types of people   Clues

_____ A person you work with; a fellow-worker.

_____ Someone who betrays their country or friends by working for an enemy.

_____ A man who is not married, or who has never been married.

_____ Someone who sees a crime being committed.

_____ A member of the armed forces _(e.g. a soldier)_ who leaves his or her post without permission and does not intend to go back.

_____ Someone who is against you in a fight or a game.

_____ A person who represents his or her country abroad.

_____ A person who rents out a room, house or flat.

_____ Someone who has chosen to live alone and to have little or no contact with other people.

_____ One of two people who are married or live together; one of the owners of a business who shares the profits and losses.

_____ One of two children born to the same mother at almost the same time.

_____ Someone who has moved abroad and now lives and/or works in a foreign country.

_____ Someone who takes a position or job previously held by someone else.

_____ Someone who rents a room in another person's house. (The owner lives there too.)

_____ Someone who has been or will be left the money, property or title of someone else when they die.

_____ Someone who rents a room, flat or house. _(From 27 Down!)_

_____ A famous person, especially an entertainer, TV or film star.

_____ Someone who helps another person to commit a crime.

_____ Someone you know, but who is not a close friend.

_____ A person or company that employs workers.

_____ Someone who pays for services or advice from a person (e.g. a solicitor) or an organisation.

_____ Someone who does not eat meat or fish.

_____ Someone who lives next door to you or near you.

_____ Someone who loves to discuss and pass on news or rumours about other people's private lives.

_____ An unusually talented or clever person.

_____ A child whose parents are both dead.

_____ A woman whose husband is dead.

_____ Someone who has been forced to leave their country, especially for political reasons or during a war.

_____ A noisy, violent person who causes trouble by fighting, etc.

_____ Someone who travels and visits places (often foreign countries) for pleasure.

_____ Someone who travels on foot, especially in an area where there are also cars.

_____ A person who is paid to work for someone else.

birds	**birthday**
book	**cake**
car	**cat**
cinema	**clothes**
doctor	**family**
fat	**film**
food	**football**
fruit	**garden**
ghost	**happy**
holiday	**hospital**

house	hungry
ill	jacket
job	library
milk	money
motorway	nervous
old	party
photograph	present
rain	restaurant
school	spider
summer	waiter

divorce (n)	complain (vb)
emigrate (vb)	hitchhike (vb)
election (n)	lonely (adj)
jealous (adj)	lazy (adj)
brochure (n)	slippery (adj)
snake (n)	arrest (vb)
exaggerate (vb)	witness (n)
rob (vb)	late (adj)
boring (adj)	profit (n)
exhausted (adj)	dictator (n)

          From *Vocabulary Games and Activities 1* by Peter Watcyn-Jones © Penguin Books 2001

Listen to the sentences, then put a circle around the word you think you hear.

1	meet	meat	11	tale	tail
2	our	hour	12	weather	whether
3	steal	steel	13	pair	pear
4	hear	here	14	sale	sail
5	stair	stare	15	wear	where
6	dear	deer	16	red	read
7	their	there	17	son	sun
8	sum	some	18	week	weak
9	flower	flour	19	way	weigh
10	right	write	20	eight	ate

---

34 The homophone game 1

Sheet 2

Read through the following sentences. Some are right and some are wrong. Decide which is which. Write right (R) or wrong (W) after each one. If wrong, underline the wrong word and say which word should have been used instead. (Do this without looking at Sheet 1.)

1 Tom, I'd like you to meat my cousin, Julia.

2 The rose is the national flower of England.

3 I always listen to the weather forecast.

4 A dog usually wags its tale when it is happy.

5 One day I'm going to sail single-handed around the world.

6 We've just come back from a weak's holiday in New York.

7 The knife is made of stainless steal.

8 There was a steep flight of stairs leading to the top floor.

9 Is that there house over their?

10 'Could I speak to Jane, please?'
   'I'm sorry. I don't know where she is at the moment.'

From *Vocabulary Games and Activities 1* by Peter Watcyn-Jones © Penguin Books 2001

35 Opposites maze

Work in pairs. See how quickly you can find your way through the maze. Start at the top with the verb **to stop** and end at the bottom with the verb **to stand up**. You should do it in ten moves only! (One pair of opposites = 1 move.)

START

to stop	to start	to laugh	to work	to play
to bring	to teach	to cry	to drink	to learn
to eat	to open	to play	to turn on	to turn off
to close	to carry	to die	to lose	to shout
to lend	to take	to win	to jump	to remember
to borrow	to ask	to answer	to whisper	to forget
to hide	to turn off	to drop	to love	to live
to help	to smoke	to hate	to follow	to die
to sink	to stay	to arrive	to say	to fly
to float	to think	to leave	to sit down	to stand up

FINISH

 From *Vocabulary Games and Activities 1* by Peter Watcyn-Jones © Penguin Books 2001

36 Board game: Categories 2

Insects	Birds
Wild animals	**Inside a house**
Fruits	**Vegetables**
Jobs & occupations	**Words to do with sleep and tiredness**
Transport/Vehicles	**Types of meat**

From *Vocabulary Games and Activities 1* by Peter Watcyn-Jones © Penguin Books 2001

36 · Board game: Categories 2

Words

lorry	ceiling	melon	lion
surgeon	(to) nod off	van	pork
stairs	beetle	eagle	peach
tram	ham	attic	spider
estate agent	cauliflower	barge	snore
bear	mosquito	lettuce	cherry
veal	hall	fox	cuckoo
drowsy	cucumber	squirrel	ant
leek	pigeon	beef	nightmare
solicitor	owl	grapes	caretaker

116 **Photocopiable**   From *Vocabulary Games and Activities 1* by Peter Watcyn-Jones © Penguin Books 2001

37 Word hunt

Work in pairs or groups of three. Name two things that:

1 are very expensive. _____

2 you can use to write with. _____

3 have a nice smell._____

4 are small enough to fit in your pocket. _____

5 are dangerous._____

6 can make you feel happy. _____

7 are thin and sharp. _____

8 you can wear above the waist. _____

9 you would find it difficult to live without. _____

10 are yellow. _____

11 make an unpleasant or loud noise. _____

12 are very heavy. _____

13 you shouldn't eat if you are on a diet. _____

14 people enjoy doing in their free time. _____

15 are found in the country (but not usually in a town). _____

16 can move very quickly._____

17 won't work without electricity. _____

18 you usually only use once. _____

19 are found in a kitchen. _____

20 people usually take with them on holiday._____

21 are containers. _____

22 you can do to stop a baby crying. _____

23 are very fragile. _____

24 can make you feel tired._____

25 people are usually frightened of. _____

26 are made of glass._____

27 taste nice._____

28 men find attractive about women (or vice-versa)._____

29 cost less than £1. _____

30 you can do to stop a nosebleed._____

From *Vocabulary Games and Activities 1* by Peter Watcyn-Jones © Penguin Books 2001 **Photocopiable** 117

38 Puzzle it out

There are five people staying at a hotel: Mr Petty, Mr Grove, Ms Williams, Ms Stevens and Mr Harvey. Use the clues to complete the chart with the information below.

Room number	101	102	103	104	105
Name					
Job					
Character					
Interest/ Hobby					
Other Information					

Job	Character	Interest/Hobby
solicitor	sociable	painting
estate agent	conceited	bird-watching
surgeon traffic	bossy	amateur dramatics
warden	mean	tennis
plumber	optimistic	gardening

Other Information

is a widower
is Australian
is a twin
is bald
is bilingual

 From *Vocabulary Games and Activities 1* by Peter Watcyn-Jones © Penguin Books 2001

38 Puzzle it out

CLUES

1   Ms Stevens usually looks on the bright side of life.

2   The man in room 101 loves going to parties and meeting people.

3   The person who works in a hospital comes from Adelaide.

4   Mr Grove doesn't like telling strangers what his job is – especially not motorists!

5   Mr Harvey sold two houses last week. The person in the room next to him often deals with divorces and wills.

6   The person who wears a uniform to work has green fingers.

7   The woman who speaks German as well as she speaks English hates spending money.

8   The tradesman has a dress rehearsal for *The Sound of Music* tonight.

9   The person who loves ordering people about has an end room.

10 Mr Harvey bought a new pair of binoculars for his hobby last weekend.

11 The estate agent's wife passed away last year.

12 Ms Williams has an excellent serve.

13 The person with a very high opinion of himself thought of buying a wig last year.

14 The person in the room next to the plumber often visits art galleries.

15 Mr Petty is in the room between Ms Stevens and Ms Williams.

16 The traffic warden's brother was born half an hour before him.

17 The optimist is staying in room 102.

18 The solicitor hopes to play at Wimbledon one day.

19 The person in room 104 never tips.

20 Mr Harvey is in room 105.

From *Vocabulary Games and Activities 1* by Peter Watcyn-Jones © Penguin Books 2001 **Photocopiable** 119

39 Matching pairs: Adjective + noun collocations

a juicy	a haunted
an urgent	a vivid
a golden	a flat
a cool	a loyal
an ambiguous	a fatal
a delicious	a tricky
a lucky/narrow	identical
an abrupt	a deadly
an infectious	an ingenious
an active	a rough

 From *Vocabulary Games and Activities 1* by Peter Watcyn-Jones © Penguin Books 2001

39 Matching pairs: Adjective + noun collocations

1 statement	**2** problem
3 ending	**4** tyre
5 disease	**6** volcano
7 orange	**8** breeze
9 meal	**10** poison
11 friend	**12** guess/estimate
13 accident	**14** message
15 escape	**16** imagination
17 plan/idea	**18** twins
19 house	**20** opportunity

40 Dominoes: Compound nouns 4

		moon	stag				

Start here →

A party for a groom and his male friends, just before the wedding.

An area of wonderful scenery.

Hamburgers, pizzas, etc. *(not healthy, easy to prepare)*

e.g. a Rolls-Royce

A place where the traffic slows down because the road becomes narrow.

A TV series with the same characters that goes on for ever!

An operation to stay young?

A sudden, clever idea.

What *Amnesty International* fights for.

Someone with no real power, e.g. the British queen – Elizabeth II.

Children v parents.

Someone who watches TV all the time.

Models walk down this at fashion shows.

A lot of killing.

An 'accidental' murder.

The state punishment for murderers. (In Britain it used to be hanging.)

A holiday for people who have just got married.

←

From *Vocabulary Games and Activities 1* by Peter Watcyn-Jones © Penguin Books 2001

40 Dominoes: Compound nouns 4

wave	human	neck	soap	walk	blood	food	status
slaughter	death	party	beauty	lift	brain	head	generation
symbol	bottle	potato	cat	penalty	honey	bath	man
rights	figure	opera	face	spot	junk	gap	couch

40 Dominoes: Compound nouns 4

Dominoes

wave	human	neck	soap	walk	blood	food	status
slaughter	death	party	beauty	lift	brain	head	generation
symbol	bottle	potato	cat	penalty	honey	bath	man
rights	figure	opera	face	spot	junk	gap	couch

generous	**cigarette**
moustache	**wedding**
big-headed	**snake**
hide	**drugs**
make a speech	**accident**
pregnant	**Good luck!**
cinema	**the USA**
hungry	**toilet**
Congratulations!	**sports car**
moustache	**excited**

 From *Vocabulary Games and Activities 1* by Peter Watcyn-Jones © Penguin Books 2001

hijack	river
dinner party	kiss
traffic warden	avalanche
ring	frightened
in love	station
Help!	thirsty
burglary	toothache
jealous	run away
wealthy	I hate you!
stubborn	overcoat

42 Vocabulary quiz: People

Quiz sheet

Team name: _____

1 Look at the drawings. Which of the three people would you describe as **skinny**?

a ☐   b ☐   c ☐

2 Is the following sentence right or wrong?

This is David. He's my **elderly** brother.   Right ☐   Wrong ☐

3 What do we call a person who works for someone else?

an employer ☐   an employee ☐

4 Which person enjoys talking about other people's private lives?

a neighbour ☐   a gossip ☐   an acquaintance ☐

5 Here are eight adjectives to describe people. Place them next to the correct heading – (four words next to each)

affectionate, bossy, cheerful, generous, greedy, mean, reliable, vain

Positive _____

Negative _____

6 She is always **punctual**. What does this mean?

She _____.

7 Which of the following is my brother's son?

my nephew ☐   my brother-in-law ☐   my niece ☐

8 She's a very **witty** person. She's _____.

clever with words ☐   good with her hands ☐   fit and strong ☐

9 We say **a troupe of dancers** and a **panel of experts**. What about the following? Match them up.

(1) a cast of (2) a team of (3) a board of (4) a staff of (5) a crew of

(a) directors (b) sailors (c) football players (d) actors (e) teachers

Write your answers here:

1	2	3	4	5	

10 Which of the following sentences is correct?

She's a very effective secretary. ☐   She's a very efficient secretary. ☐

Photocopiable   From *Vocabulary Games and Activities 1* by Peter Watcyn-Jones © Penguin Books 2001

11 What sort of a person do you think of when you hear these words?

hospital, check-up, prescription, stethoscope Your answer: _____

12 Fill in the missing preposition in this sentence.

My uncle is very prejudiced _____ foreigners.

13 Rearrange the letters in the word at the end of this sentence to form a word that means 'a child whose both parents are dead' **naphor**

Your answer: _____

14 My sister is a very **brave** person. What's the opposite of 'brave'?
c_____

15 Below are definitions of four types of people. Who are they? Choose from the following:

a survivor, a hooligan, a victim, a bachelor, a refugee, a spectator, a hermit, a colleague

1 An unmarried man. (_____)

2 A person who lives apart from (and avoids) other people. (_____)

3 A person who has been forced to leave his/her country for political reasons.

(_____)

4 A person who causes damage and is noisy and violent in public places.

(_____)

16 Which person is the 'odd one out'?

widow □   mother-in-law □   uncle □   fiancée □

17 Which person would be most likely to say: 'Anything to declare?'

_____

18 Look at the drawing.
Which word would you
use to describe the woman?

She's ... excited □   pregnant □   overweight □

19 Janice is very **stubborn**. What is a synonym for 'stubborn'?
strict □   big-headed □   obstinate □

20 Look at the eight verbs in the boxes. Choose five that are to do with physical contact between people.

hug □	wade □	tickle □	bribe □
pinch □	stare □	kiss □	cuddle □

TOTAL SCORE: _____

43 Half a crossword: Verbs

Work in groups A and B. You are A.

Some of the words in the following crossword are missing. Group B know what they are. Group B also have some words that are missing from their crossword. They are the words at the bottom of the page.

Take it in turns to ask each other for a missing word. You can ask: **What's (2) Across? What's (3) Down?** etc.

Here are the words you will have to explain for Group B.

admire	envy	invent	quote	survive
bribe	exaggerate	nag	refuse	
deny	force	obey	satisfy	
encourage	hesitate	pollute	sneeze	

Photocopiable   From *Vocabulary Games and Activities 1* by Peter Watcyn-Jones © Penguin Books 2001

43 Half a crossword: Verbs

Work in groups A and B. You are B.

Some of the words in the following crossword are missing. Group A know what they are. Group A also have some words that are missing from their crossword. They are the words at the bottom of the page.

Take it in turns to ask each other for a missing word. You can ask: **What's (7) Across? What's (1) Down?** etc.

Here are the words you will have to explain for Group A.

abolish	cure	execute	play truant	tow
afford	dare	gossip	recognise	
annoy	discover	oversleep	replace	
boast	estimate	overtake	suspect	

From *Vocabulary Games and Activities 1* by Peter Watcyn-Jones © Penguin Books 2001   **Photocopiable**   129

44 Half a crossword: Adjectives to describe people

Work in groups A and B. You are A.

Some of the words in the following crossword are missing. Group B know what they are. Group B also have some words that are missing from their crossword. They are the words at the bottom of the page.

Take it in turns to ask each other for a missing word. You can ask: **What's (3) Across? What's (2) Down?** etc.

Here are the words you will have to explain for Group B.

bossy	handsome	lazy	polite	selfish
cruel	irresponsible	mean	punctual	sensitive
friendly	jealous	modest	reliable	witty

 From *Vocabulary Games and Activities 1* by Peter Watcyn-Jones © Penguin Books 2001

44 Half a crossword: Adjectives to describe people
Group B

Work in groups A and B. You are B.

Some of the words in the following crossword are missing. Group A know what they are. Group A also have some words that are missing from their crossword. They are the words at the bottom of the page.

Take it in turns to ask each other for a missing word. You can ask: **What's (7) Across? What's (1) Down?** etc.

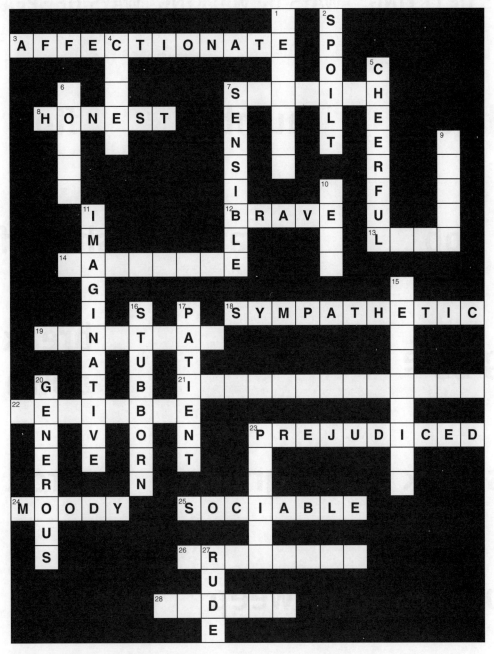

Here are the words you will have to explain for Group A.

affectionate	generous	moody	rude	spoilt
brave	honest	patient	sensible	stubborn
cheerful	imaginative	prejudiced	sociable	sympathetic

From *Vocabulary Games and Activities 1* by Peter Watcyn-Jones © Penguin Books 2001

Photocopiable   131

45 Group the words: Verbs

WAYS OF HITTING	WAYS OF LAUGHING/ SMILING	WAYS OF STEALING
WAYS OF CRYING	WAYS OF WALKING	WAYS OF SPEAKING
chuckle	mumble	flog
sob	beat	shoplift
giggle	recite	break down
smack	grin	stroll
burgle	weep	hike
rob	march	chat

 From *Vocabulary Games and Activities 1* by Peter Watcyn-Jones © Penguin Books 2001

46 Phrasal verb maze

Work in pairs. Fill in the missing phrasal verbs in each sentence to get though the maze in twenty moves. (To help you, the first square has already been filled in.) You will end up in one of the boxes in the last row.

START

turn up	look into	go off	call on	call off
look through	take up	blow up	try out	look up
fall out	break out	put up with	take after	take to
bring up	hold up	get over	break away	call for
drop out	come into	take over	bring out	give up
put up	take off	look up to	break down	break up
carry on	fall out	go with	go out	get on
go over	drop off	put off	look down on	get by
hold on	bring back	turn back	turn down	drop out
cut off	look after	pick up	put on	go up

FINISH

From *Vocabulary Games and Activities 1* by Peter Watcyn-Jones © Penguin Books 2001

46 Phrasal verb maze

Fill in the missing phrasal verbs in each sentence to find a way though the maze.
To help you, the first square has already been filled in. (The sentences are in the
correct order!)

1   She was late and didn't **turn up** until 11.30. *(arrive)*

2   The boss asked me to _____ the complaints we had received. *(investigate)*

3   The soldiers tried to _____ the bridge. *(destroy with explosives)*

4   I never buy anything unless I _____ it _____ first. *(test)*

5   Because the lead singer was ill, they had to _____ the concert. *(cancel)*

6   If you don't know what the word means, then _____ it _____ in a
    dictionary. *(try to find its meaning)*

7   What a lovely baby! Does he _____ you or your husband? *(look like,
    resemble)*

8   I think it's going to take Joanna quite a while to _____ her illness. *(recover
    from)*

9   Two masked men _____ a bank in the centre of Manchester early this
    morning. They got away with nearly £20,000. *(robbed)*

10 When her father dies, Paula will _____ quite a lot of money. *(inherit)*

11 There are very few politicians you can _____ these days, aren't there?
    (respect and admire)

12 They are planning to _____ a new Internet magazine next month
    especially for pensioners. *(publish)*

13 It's very easy to _____ smoking. I've done it hundreds of times! *(stop)*

14 When do British schools _____ for the summer? *(close for the holidays)*

15 I _____ really well with my mother-in-law. Better, in fact, than with my
    own mother. *(have a very good relationship with)*

16 Put some more wood on the fire, Paul. We don't want it to _____ yet, do
    we? *(stop burning)*

17 'Does that dress _____ my eyes, do you think?' *(match)*
    'Which dress – the red or the blue one?'

18 We decided to _____ the meeting until the following week. *(postpone)*

19 This is an offer you really can't afford to _____. *(refuse)*

20 I really must go on a diet. I've _____ at least three kilos in the past two
    months. *(gained in weight)*

 From *Vocabulary Games and Activities 1* by Peter Watcyn-Jones © Penguin Books 2001

48 20-square: Explain the words

Sentences

1 a *huge* garden	**2** a *priceless* painting	**3** a terrible *earthquake*	**4** to *limp* along the street
5 a pleasant *chat*	**6** a *temporary* job	**7** a £10,000 *ransom*	**8** the *average* salary
9 a face full of *freckles*	**10** to *call off* a meeting	**11** an ugly *scar*	**12** a terrible *pessimist*
13 to *fall out* with a friend	**14** a *plump* woman	**15** an *exhausting* day	**16** a successful *barrister*
17 a *courageous* soldier	**18** to feel *embarrassed*	**19** a £1 million *loss*	**20** the only *survivor*

49 Find someone who ... 3

Find someone who:

1 knows what **trunk**, **bark** and **branch** are connected with.

2 knows what an **optician** does.

3 knows two synonyms for **awful**.

4 knows where British people would wear a **vest**.

5 knows what someone suffering from **insomnia** has trouble in doing.

6 can give the British words for the following American ones.

   drapes   c_____

   closet   w_____

   gasoline p_____

7 can think of five words that start with **dis-**.

8 can give one word for each of the following definitions:

   not sharp (e.g. a knife)

   b____

   bad-mannered, impolite

   r____

   that cannot be seen

   i____

9 can say what this is:

10 can explain the expression **to pull someone's leg**.

11 can give two synonyms or words that are similar in meaning to the verb **hate**.

12 can think of five words that start with **par-**.

13 knows who would use **handcuffs**.

14 can explain the difference between **recipe** and **receipt**.

15 can name two **natural disasters** (e.g. flood).

16 knows what a **gate-crasher** is.

17 knows three words to do with **computers**.

18 can say which of the following is called a **beetle**.

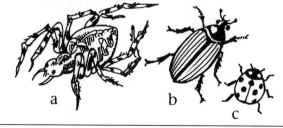

19 can think of three words that rhyme with **key**.

20 knows where you would find an **attic**.

     From *Vocabulary Games and Activities 1* by Peter Watcyn-Jones © Penguin Books 2001

50 Sort out the punch lines

In the following twelve jokes, the punch lines have got mixed up. See if you can work out which punch line belongs to which joke.

Joke 1

Man If you really are a police officer, then why on earth are you wearing that red and yellow patterned suit?

Policeman Oh dear! What shape should it be, then?

Joke 2

Ironmonger Can I help you, sir?

Customer I'd like a mousetrap, please. And hurry, I've got a bus to catch.

Ironmonger It's too late now – it's flown away!

Joke 3

Boy I say, what a lovely coloured cow over there.

Girl It's a Jersey.

Boy Don't be stupid! That's the new rabbit hutch!

Joke 4

Customer I'll have four nice pork chops, please. And make them lean.

Butcher All right. Here's a paper bag.

Joke 5

Mechanic The trouble with your car is simple, sir. The battery's flat.

Man Oh, I didn't know it was electric.

Joke 6

Woman My budgie lays square eggs.

Man That's amazing! Can it talk as well?

Woman Yes, but only one word.

Man What's that?

Woman Sorry, sir – we don't make them that big.

Joke 7

Child There's a man outside with a big, bushy beard.

Father Is it a naval beard?

Child Just a routine check, sir.

Joke 8

Patient Doctor, my hair's falling out. I want something to keep it in.

Doctor Certainly, sir. Which way?

Joke 9

It was the Royal wedding.

Father Where's your mum?

Daughter She's upstairs waving her hair.

Father Ouch!

Joke 10

Neighbour How's your wife?

Man Oh, she's ill. She's very, very ill.

Neighbour Oh, I'm sorry to hear that. Is that her coughing?

Man No, it grows on his chin.

Joke 11

Salesman Right, here's your new bath, madam. Do you want a plug for it?

Woman Can't we afford a flag?

Joke 12

Boy Dad! Dad! I've been stung by a wasp.

Dad Don't worry, son. I'll put some special cream on it.

Boy Really? I thought it was its skin.

advertise	ambitious
astrology	bald
bargain	boring
cheeky	conference
cruise	depressed
disappointed	drugs
earthquake	Eiffel Tower
elephant	envious
feel sorry for	fiancé(e)
generation gap	get the sack

 From Vocabulary Games and Activities 1 by Peter Watcyn-Jones © Penguin Books 2001

headline	housework
illegal	line-dancing
lonely	on strike
overweight	postpone
president	receipt
refugee	rubber plant
scared	shy
spaghetti	steal
surgeon	unemployed
weekend	wig

52 Make two words

Find two letters that will complete the word on the left and start the word on the right.

1	w	o	m		s	w	e	r
2		b	o		t	a	c	k
3		c	a	b		v	e	n	t
4	b	l	o	u		c	r	e	t
5	c	e	n	t		a	s	o	n
6			c	l		p	e	a	r
7	y	e	l	l		n	e	r
8		e	a	g		a	t	h	e	r
9	p	r	e	t		r	e
10		t	o	a		r	e	a	m
11		c	r	e		o	u	n	t
12		s	p	o		i	o	n
13			o	p		e	m	y
14		p	i	l		h	e	r
15	c	a	m	e		i	n
16		r	e	a		o	i	r

Fold

| se |
| ch |
| st |
| en |
| le |
| ra |
| ap |
| on |
| at |
| re |
| ot |
| in |
| am |
| ow |
| an |
| ty |

Photocopiable   From *Vocabulary Games and Activities 1* by Peter Watcyn-Jones © Penguin Books 2001

53 Half a crossword: Crime, law and order
Group A

Work in groups A and B. You are A.

Some of the words in the following crossword are missing. Group B know what they are. Group B also have some words that are missing from their crossword. They are the words at the bottom of the page.

Take it in turns to ask each other for a missing word. You can ask: **What's (1) Across? What's (4) Down?** etc.

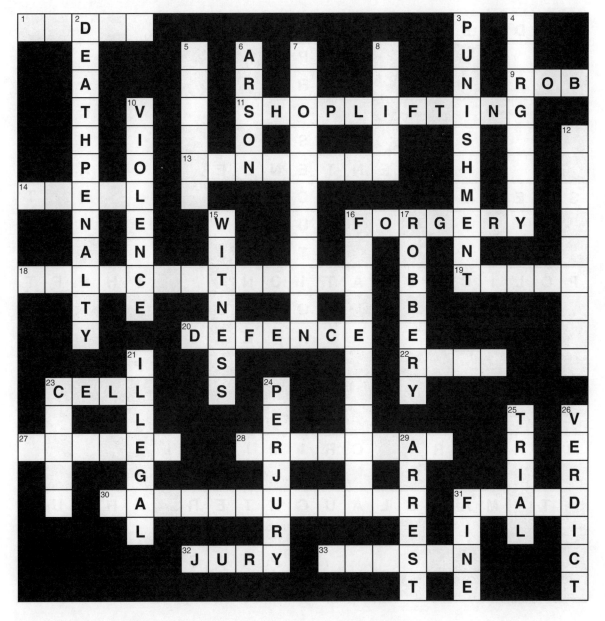

Here are the words you will have to explain for Group B.

arrest	defence	jury	robbery	violence
arson	fine	perjury	shoplifting	witness
cell	forgery	punishment	trial	
death penalty	illegal	rob	verdict	

From *Vocabulary Games and Activities 1* by Peter Watcyn-Jones © Penguin Books 2001

Photocopiable 141

53 Half a crossword: Crime, law and order

Work in groups A and B. You are B.

Some of the words in the following crossword are missing. Group A know what they are. Group A also have some words that are missing from their crossword. They are the words at the bottom of the page.

Take it in turns to ask each other for a missing word. You can ask: **What's (9) Across? What's (2) Down?** etc.

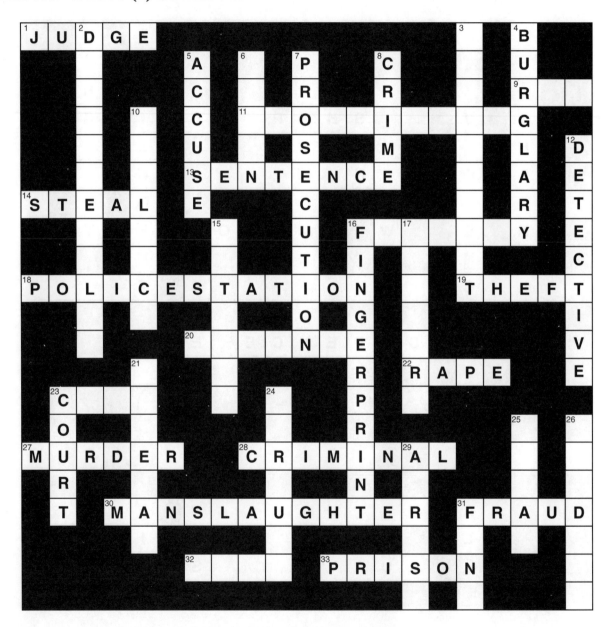

Here are the words you will have to explain for Group A.

accuse	criminal	judge	prison	steal
burglary	detective	manslaughter	prosecution	theft
court	fingerprint	murder	rape	
crime	fraud	police station	sentence	

 From *Vocabulary Games and Activities 1* by Peter Watcyn-Jones © Penguin Books 2001

54 Sort out the clues: Health words

In this crossword, all the words have been filled in. Sort out which clue goes with each word. Write the correct answer (1 Down, 8 Across, etc.) in front of each clue. Then arrange them in two columns with the Across clues on the left and the Down clues on the right.

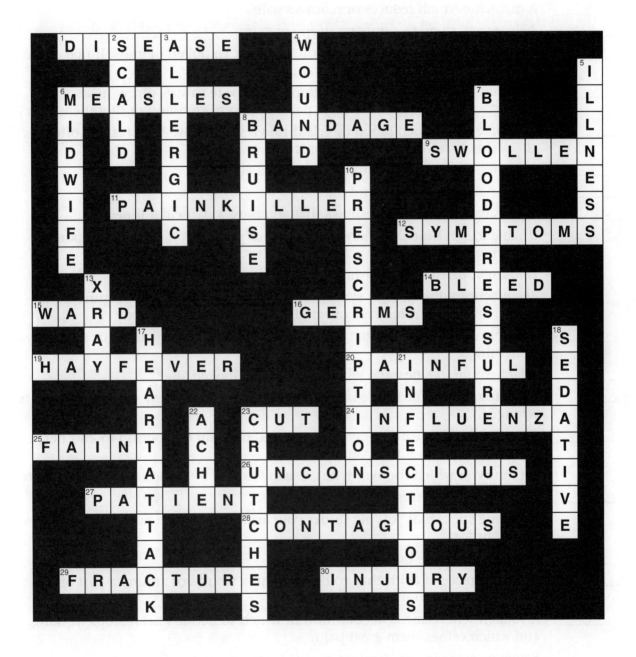

54 Sort out the clues: Health words
Clues

_____ A piece of paper on which a doctor writes what medicine a sick person should have.

_____ To lose blood, especially because of an injury.

_____ A specially trained nurse who helps women when they are having a baby.

_____ To suddenly become unconscious.

_____ A wound, or damage to part of your body, caused by an accident or an attack.

_____ If a disease or illness is this, it means that it can be passed on from one person to another, especially through the air that you breathe.

_____ A medicine which reduces or removes pain.

_____ A drug used to make someone sleepy or calm.

_____ A medical condition where a person is allergic to pollen or grass. It makes the person sneeze, makes their eyes water, etc.

_____ An illness that gives you a high temperature, sore throat, runny nose, headache, dry cough, and muscle pain. (It is very common during the winter.)

_____ The force with which blood travels through your body. A doctor will often check this to see if it is too high or too low.

_____ An illness, e.g. measles, mumps, smallpox, etc.

_____ A dull pain that goes on and on.

_____ A physical condition that shows that you have a particular illness.

_____ Unable to see, hear, or otherwise sense what is going on, usually temporarily and often as a result of an accident or injury.

_____ To burn yourself with very hot liquid.

_____ An infectious disease with symptoms that include a high temperature, sore throat, and a bright red rash of small spots over the whole body.

_____ A purple or brown mark that you get on your skin when you fall or are hit by something.

_____ A large room in a hospital where patients are looked after.

_____ A photograph of the inside of a person's body. It is taken to see if something is wrong.

_____ The kind of disease or illness can be passed on from one person to another, especially through direct contact.

_____ An injury in which the skin is cut, usually caused by an accident, violence, etc.

_____ Causing pain; hurting.

_____ Two long sticks that you put under your arms to help you walk when you have hurt your leg.

_____ To break or crack a bone.

_____ A narrow piece of cloth that you tie around a wound or around a part of the body that has been injured.

_____ A sudden serious medical condition in which someone's heart stops working, and which causes them great pain.

_____ Someone receiving medical treatment from a doctor.

_____ Being very sensitive to a substance (e.g. cat's hair), so it can make you ill.

_____ A skin wound, usually made with a knife, piece of glass, etc.

_____ Bacteria (small living organisms) that can cause disease.

_____ A disease of the body or mind.

_____ If a part of your body is this, then it is bigger than usual because of illness or injury.

 From Vocabulary Games and Activities 1 by Peter Watcyn-Jones © Penguin Books 2001

55 Matching pairs: Parts of the body idioms

A-cards

to be all fingers and thumbs

to catch someone's eye

to get cold feet

to give someone the cold shoulder

to have a chip on your shoulder

to have green fingers

to make your blood boil

to pay through the nose for something

to pull someone's leg

to put your foot in it

to stick your neck out

to stretch your legs

From *Vocabulary Games and Activities 1* by Peter Watcyn-Jones © Penguin Books 2001

Photocopiable 145

55 Matching pairs: Parts of the body idioms

to have a grievance/an inferiority complex about something	1
to cause embarrassment by saying something tactless	2
to be clumsy	3
to be good at gardening	4
to ignore someone	5
to attract someone's attention	6
to tease someone	7
to go for a walk	8
to take a risk	9
to pay too much for something	10
to lose courage/ to be afraid to do something	11
to make you very angry	12

 From *Vocabulary Games and Activities 1* by Peter Watcyn-Jones © Penguin Books 2001

56 What does it mean?

Listen and write the numbers 1-16 in the box next to the correct speech bubbles.

1	2	3	4	5
6	7	8	9	10
11	12	13	14	15
16	17	18	19	20
21	22	23	24	25
26	27	28	29	30

From *Vocabulary Games and Activities 1* by Peter Watcyn-Jones © Penguin Books 2001

57 Board game: Three-in-a-row

Square 1

It's quite unbelievable. Which word beginning with *i* is a synonym for *unbelievable*?

ANSWER: **incredible**

What's the piece of glass in a window called? It starts with the letter *p*.

ANSWER: **a pane**

Square 2

What word in English do we use to describe such things as ghosts, flying saucers, telepathy and so on – things that can't be explained naturally? The ____. What?

ANSWER: **the supernatural**

If you are feeling *dead beat* you are: hungry / very tired / ill

ANSWER: **very tired**

Square 3

Which of the following is correct? Take your seats please, the play is about to start. / Take your places please, the play is about to start.

ANSWER: **seats**

Is this right or wrong? (*At the theatre*) There will be a fifteen-minute pause between Acts one and two.

ANSWER: **Wrong. It should be interval.**

Square 4

If you felt peckish, what would you feel like doing?

ANSWER: **Eating. It means you are slightly hungry.**

To help you to understand a foreign programme on television, you often have words underneath the picture. What are these words called?

ANSWER: **subtitles**

Square 5

Is this right or wrong? Lying in the sun can often make you feel rather drowsy.

ANSWER: **Right. It means slightly tired or sleepy.**

Which of the following words is the odd one out?
circulation / leader / column / channel

ANSWER: **channel (the others are to do with a newspaper)**

Square 6

What do we call a person who lives in one town but travels to another town to work? It starts with *c*.

ANSWER: **a commuter**

Which of the following words is a synonym for *obstinate*?
mean / stubborn / affectionate

ANSWER: **stubborn**

Square 7

How might you feel if you looked down from the top of a very high building?

ANSWER: **dizzy/giddy (Accept other answers if they make sense.)**

What do you think of when you hear the words *bark, trunk, willow* and *branch*?

ANSWER: **a tree**

Square 8

Which of the following is a synonym for *hate*?
disgust / loathe / deter

ANSWER: **loathe**

Which of the following means *they quarrelled*? They fell apart. / They fell through. / They fell out.

ANSWER: **They fell out.**

Square 9

Which word beginning with *b* do we use to describe a person who can speak two languages fluently?

ANSWER: **bilingual**

This disease can be passed on by touch. What word do we use to describe this? This disease is ____. What? It starts with *c*.

ANSWER: **contagious**

Square 10

If you are broke, this means that you don't have any ____. What?

ANSWER: **money**

Which of these is correct? Is there space in the car for me as well? / Is there room in the car for me as well?

ANSWER: **room**

Square 11

What do we call someone who can't read or write? It starts with *i*.

ANSWER: **illiterate**

Which of the following is not an insect: beetle / cockerel / ant / ladybird

ANSWER: **cockerel (= young chicken, cock)**

Square 12

Which word means to run away secretly in order to get married – usually without the permission of one's parents? It starts with *e*.

ANSWER: **elope**

What could you say instead of *the dog attacked him*?
The dog went away with him. / The dog went in for him. / The dog went for him.

ANSWER: **went for**

Square 13

Which of the following people would use an easel? an artist / a photographer / an electrician

ANSWER: **an artist**

Which word beginning with *e* means to listen secretly to a private conversation?

ANSWER: **eavesdrop**

Square 14

What is the missing preposition in the following sentence? He hates losing ____ cards.

ANSWER: **at**

What does the expression *to thumb a lift* mean?

ANSWER: **to hitchhike**

Square 15

Which speaker might be slightly frightened? I was startled. / I was amazed. / I was astounded.

ANSWER: **I was startled.**

The words *diamonds, spades* and *deal* all have something to do with ____. What?

ANSWER: **cards/playing cards**

57 Board game: Three-in-a-row

Square 16

Which of the following people would use a baton? a policeman / a conductor / an undertaker

ANSWER: **a conductor. (S/He holds it when s/he conducts.)**

If a friend says he can *put you up* this means he can: give you a lift home / offer you somewhere to sleep / lend you a ladder

ANSWER: **offer you somewhere to sleep**

Square 17

Dawn is the time of day when light first appears. What do we call the time of day when daylight is fading?

ANSWER: **dusk/twilight**

Which word beginning with *a* means to murder a ruler or a politician for political reasons or reward?

ANSWER: **assassinate**

Square 18

Which of the following is not part of a car? a boot / a bonnet / a deck / a clutch

ANSWER: **a deck (part of a ship)**

The water is very deep here. What's the opposite of deep?

ANSWER: **shallow**

Square 19

Which of the following is an example of crockery? a cup / a banana / a knife / a nephew

ANSWER: **a cup**

All these words mean *to pull*, but which do we use when one car is pulling another?
to haul / to tug / to tow

ANSWER: **to tow**

Square 20

Which of these is a place where a river meets the sea? a gulf / a bay / an estuary / an inlet

ANSWER: **an estuary**

All these are sounds we make when we are amused. Which is the loudest? a giggle / a chuckle / a guffaw

ANSWER: **a guffaw**

Square 21

Finish this proverb. As old as _____. Samson / the hills / dry bread

ANSWER: **the hills**

Which of these is nearest in meaning to *to put up with*? to tolerate / to permit / to allow

ANSWER: **to tolerate**

Square 22

Your nearest relative is your _____. What? closest kin / first kin / next of kin

ANSWER: **next of kin**

In Britain where might you see the sign 'To let'? outside a house / on a car / inside a hotel

ANSWER: **outside a house**

Square 23

An American says *period* when a British person says _____. What? semi-colon / colon / full stop

ANSWER: **full stop**

An American says *streetcar* when a British person says _____. What? tram / family car / coach

ANSWER: **tram**

Square 24

Give another word for *drawback*. It also starts with *d*.

ANSWER: **disadvantage**

A bird in the hand is worth two in the _____. What?
tree / bush / forest

ANSWER: **bush**

Square 25

An American says *freeway* when a British person says _____. What? main road / dual carriageway / motorway

ANSWER: **motorway**

An American talks about *a janitor* when a British person says _____. What? a cleaner / a porter / a caretaker

ANSWER: **a caretaker**

Square 26

Who would you expect to use handcuffs?

ANSWER: **a police officer (You put them around a prisoner's wrists.)**

What do we call a child who hits smaller or weaker children? It starts with *b*.

ANSWER: **a bully**

Square 27

If you were suspicious, you might say *I smell a _____*. What? cat / horse / rat

ANSWER: **rat**

Is a cockroach an insect or a bird?

ANSWER: **an insect**

Square 28

Is the following True or False? I hate the flat I'm living in at the moment. I'm really homesick.

ANSWER: **False. Homesick means that you are unhappy away from home.**

Is a magpie a fish or a bird?

ANSWER: **a bird**

Square 29

Which animal trumpets? a duck / an elephant / a bull

ANSWER: **an elephant**

Is your instep part of your hand / arm / foot?

ANSWER: **Your foot. It's the middle part of the foot from the toes to the ankle.**

Square 30

If you're suffering from insomnia, what do you have difficulty in doing? eating / sleeping / walking

ANSWER: **sleeping**

Where would you find portholes? on a car / on an aeroplane / on a ship

ANSWER: **on an aeroplane. They're the round windows.**

 From *Vocabulary Games and Activities 1* by Peter Watcyn-Jones © Penguin Books 2001

58 Board game: Verbs

Verbs to do with looking	**Verbs to do with walking/running**
Verbs to do with speaking/listening	**Verbs to do with holding/pulling**
Verbs to do with facial expressions	**Verbs to do with sounds people/animals make**
Verbs to do with shining/burning	**Verbs to do with violence/death**

bleat	stare	hug	stagger
scald	mug	tug	jog
singe	neigh	lisp	smile
stroll	stab	grin	leer
pass away	peep	mumble	glance
bark	beat up	dash	drag
eavesdrop	flicker	frown	gaze
glow	grasp	twinkle	tow
hiccup	limp	overhear	squint
pout	stammer	assassinate	snore

 From *Vocabulary Games and Activities 1* by Peter Watcyn-Jones © Penguin Books 2001

59 New words from old

Which noun can you add to all four words to form new single-word nouns or two-word nouns?

(Note: the noun can be added before or after the word.)

Example: hand**bag**, kit**bag**, **bag**pipes, sleeping **bag**

1 band, chair, fire, pit   _____

2 end, guide, mark, scrap   _____

3 board, Christmas, credit, score   _____

4 hanger, over, rain, waist   _____

5 candle, flood, house, sky   _____

6 clip, news, wall, weight   _____

7 battle, friend, space, wreck   _____

8 fall, proof, salt, melon   _____

9 basket, eye, snow, room   _____

10 bath, service, class, changing   _____

11 arm, woman, push, wheel   _____

12 guest, hold, boarding, wife   _____

13 box, card, goal, lamp   _____

14 room, cup, dash, key   _____

15 head, coast, dead, up   _____

16 cloth, coffee, spoon, time   _____

17 page, cow, friend, hood   _____

18 father, foot, ladder, in   _____

19 chatter, gear, room, post   _____

20 flower, coffee, hole, tea   _____

60 Vocabulary quiz: Idioms

Team name: _____

1   Is the following sentence right or wrong?

He hasn't long left school. This is his first job. He's still a bit **wet behind the ears**.
Right ☐   Wrong ☐

2   Which of the following words could be used to describe a book?

thick-skinned ☐   dog-eared ☐   stiff-necked ☐

3   Which word beginning with the letter 'g' means 'someone who goes to a party that he/she hasn't been invited to'? a g_____

4   Look at the following drawing.

What do we call the lines or wrinkles the arrow is pointing to? You need two words for your answer. The first word is a bird and the second word is a part of the body.

Your answer: _____'s _____

5   My uncle has recently **kicked the bucket**. What has happened to him?

He has _____.

6   Which person is suspicious about something?

'I smell a rat.' ☐   'I'm in a rut.' ☐   'I'm in two minds about it.' ☐

7   If a man was slightly bald, he might say 'I'm a bit _____ on top.'

loose ☐   thin ☐   empty ☐

8   Place the following idioms next to the correct heading – (two under each)

hair-raising, have a screw loose, have kittens, hot under the collar, off one's head, throw a wobbly

Madness/Insanity: _____

Fear: _____

Anger: _____

9   Which part of the body best completes this idiom?

To get a flat in the centre of this town you have to pay through the _____ for it.

Your answer: _____

 From *Vocabulary Games and Activities 1* by Peter Watcyn-Jones © Penguin Books 2001

10 What do people usually talk about when they **talk shop**?

  _____

11 Which of the following would be the most useful thing for a politician to have?

  a white elephant ☐   a tight squeeze ☐   the gift of the gab ☐

12 He gave a speech without preparing for it. He spoke _____.

  on the spur of the moment ☐   off the cuff ☐   at the eleventh hour ☐

13 If a couple share the cost of a meal in a restaurant, they go _____.

  British ☐   French ☐   Dutch ☐

14 Peter's **behind bars**. Where is he? _____

15 Complete the following proverbs and sayings.

  (a) A rolling s_____ gathers no moss.

  (b) A bird in the hand is worth t_____ in the bush.

  (c) P____ makes perfect.

  (d) Every cloud has a s____ lining.

  (e) Out of the frying pan and into the f_____.

  Your answers:

  (a) _____   (b) _____   (c) _____

  (d) _____   (e) _____

16 Which of the following idioms would best describe an older woman trying to look and dress like a much younger one?

  a sight for sore eyes ☐   mutton dressed as lamb ☐   no spring chicken ☐

17 Complete this expression: 'As keen as _____.'

  a cucumber ☐   mustard ☐   cornflakes ☐

18 The exam was a **piece of cake**. What does this mean?

  It was easy. ☐   It was difficult. ☐   It was enjoyable. ☐

19 Which of the following is most likely to be **hen-pecked**?

  a pregnant woman ☐   someone in love ☐   a husband ☐

20 Look at the eight idioms in the boxes. Choose five that are to do with money.

hard up ☐	caught up ☐	make ends meet ☐	a skinflint ☐
on the mend ☐	in the red ☐	polish off ☐	a nest-egg ☐

TOTAL SCORE: _____

Numbers 1–20

1	2	3	4
(one)	(two)	(three)	(four)
5	6	7	8
(five)	(six)	(seven)	(eight)
9	10	11	12
(nine)	(ten)	(eleven)	(twelve)
13	14	15	16
(thirteen)	(fourteen)	(fifteen)	(sixteen)
17	18	19	20
(seventeen)	(eighteen)	(nineteen)	(twenty)

 From *Vocabulary Games and Activities 1* by Peter Watcyn-Jones © Penguin Books 2001

How to define words

Here are some words and phrases you can use when you try to give a definition of
a word.

General

It's …	a noun, an adjective, a verb, an adverb, etc.

Things/objects

It's …	blue, red, green, etc.
	round, square, oval, etc.
	big, small, fairly big, very small, etc.
	made of … (wood, plastic, glass, etc.)
	something you … (wear, eat, drink, etc.)
	a feeling, a part of the body, etc.
It's a (type of) …	tree, weapon, container, bird, flower, musical instrument, sport, etc.
It's part of …	a car, a bicycle, a computer, etc.
You use it …	to cook with, to look up a word, to wake you up in the morning when you swim, when you wash, when you eat, etc.
It's used …	for reading, for playing football, for writing, etc.

People

It's someone who …	works in a (hotel, bank, theatre, school, etc.)
Its a person who …	helps people when they are ill, stops you from parking your car in the wrong place, etc.
This person …	is often ill, wears a uniform, is in charge of a company, etc.
He/She …	has committed a crime, flies an aeroplane, etc.
It's …	a relative, a type of … (criminal, soldier, politician, etc.)

Verbs

It's a way of …	walking, eating, speaking, moving, etc.
It means to …	drive past another car, laugh in a very loud way, etc.
It's another word for …	hit, look, talk, etc.
It's the opposite of …	arrive, sell, win, etc.

Adjectives

It's how you feel when you …	are very tired, have just passed an exam, really looking forward to something, very hungry, etc.
It's another word for …	sad, big, happy, afraid, etc.
It's the opposite of …	sad, old, rough, sharp, etc.

Key words

The number after each of the words/phrases refers to the game or activity where the words/phrases appear.

AmE = American English

a bar of chocolate 24
a bird in the hand is worth two in the bush 57, 60
A bottle of cough medicine, please. 28
a bottle of milk 24
a box of matches 24
A first-class stamp, please. 28
a packet of biscuits 24
a rolling stone gathers no moss
a sight for sore eyes 60
A single to Brighton, please. 28
a tin of soup 24
A wash and blow-dry, please. 28
abolish 43
abrupt ending 39
accident 41
accomplice 31
accuse 53
ache 54
acquaintance 31, 42
action verbs 10
Action! 28
active volcano 39
actor 8
address 12
adjectives 10
admire 43
advertise 51
advertisement 30
aeroplane (plane) 9, 23
affectionate 42, 44, 57
afford 43
afraid 22
alarm clock 7
allergic 54
allowed–aloud 47
alphabet 14
amateur dramatics 38
amazed 57
amazing 50
ambassador 31
ambiguous statement 39
ambitious 51
amount 52
animal 13
annoy 43
answer 35, 52
answer the phone 16
ant 36, 57
Any more fares, please? 28
Anything to declare? 28
apartment (AmE) 27
appear 52
apple 6, 10, 24
Are you being served? 28
Are you English? 5
armband 59
armchair 7, 59
armpit 59
arrest 53

arrive 35
arson 53
as keen as mustard
as old as the hills 57
ashtray 1, 18, 25
ask 35
ask a question 16
assassinate 57, 58
astounded 57
astrology 51
at the eleventh hour
athletics 19
attack 52
attic 30, 36, 49
attractive 37
aunt, 9
Australian 38
autumn 27
avalanche 30, 41
average 48
awful 26, 49
baby 8
bachelor 31, 42
back, 10
bacon and eggs 24
bad 15
bad-mannered 49
badminton 19
bag 1
baker 13, 24
bald 38, 51
ballroom 59
banana 6, 10, 24
bandage 54
bar 30
bargain 29, 39, 51
barge 36
bark (animal sound) 58
bark (tree) 49, 57
barrister 48
basketball 18, 59
bathroom 7, 13, 21, 25, 59
baton 57
battleship 59
bay 57
be a bit thin on top 56, 60
be a piece of cake 60
be all fingers and thumbs 55
be behind bars 60
be given the sack 56
be hard up 60
be hen-pecked 60
be hot under the collar 60
be in a rut 56, 60
be in two minds about something 60
be off one's head 60
be over the moon 56
be taken for a ride 56
be tickled pink 56
be wet behind the ears 60
bear 36
bear–bare 47
beard 30

beat 45
beat up 58
beautiful 10
beauty spot 40
bed 3, 10, 21
bedroom 13, 18, 21
bedroom furniture 25
bee 23
beech 25
beef 36
beetle 36, 49, 57
belt 11
bicycle (bike) 9
big 13, 15
big-headed 41, 42
bilingual 38, 57
bill (restaurant) 27
binoculars 38
bird 23, 36
birds 32
bird-watching 38
birthday 12, 32
birthday card 59
biscuit 1
black 10
bleat 58
bleed 54
blonde 12
blood pressure 54
bloodbath 40
blouse 52
blow one's top 56
blow up 46
blow your nose 16
blue 10, 22
board of director 42s
board–bored 47
boarding house 59
boardroom 59
boast 43
boat 23, 52
bonnet 57
book 3, 23, 32
bookcase 7, 10
bookend 59
bookmark 59
boot (of a car) 57
boots 11
boring 33, 51
borrow 12, 35
boss 8
bossy 38, 42, 44
bottle 3
bottleneck 40
bowl 24, 25
box room 59
boxing 19
boyfriend 59
boyhood 59
brainwave 40
branch 49, 57
brave 42, 44
Brazil 24l
bread 6, 24
break down 45

break up 46
breakfast 22, 24
bribe 42, 43
bridge 10
briefcase 18, 23
bring 35
bring out 46
brochure 33
broke (= no money) 57
brother 8
brother-in-law 42
bruise 54
brush my teeth 4
brush your teeth 16
bucket 30
budgie 50
build a house 16
building 9, 25
bully 57
burglary 30, 41, 53
burgle 45
bus 9
bus driver 8
bus stop 10
bushes 21
business 25
busker 25
butcher 13, 24
butterfly 18
cab (AmE) 27
cabbage 24
cabin 52
cage 30
cake 6, 32
cakes 24
call off 46, 48
camera 3, 14, 52
camping 19
can (AmE) 27
Can I have the bill, please? 24
Can I help you? (in a shop) 17
Can you help me, please? 5
candlelight 59
candy (AmE) 27
capital 12
car 9, 23, 32
car park 7, 27
caravan 25
card 14
cardboard 59
caretaker 36, 57
carrot 1, 10, 14, 24
carry 35
cash 30
cast of actors 42
cat 12, 32
catch a bus 50
catch a cold 16
catch someone's eye 55
catwalk 40
cauliflower 36
ceiling 36
celebrity 31

PENGUIN ENGLISH PHOTOCOPIABLES

0 582 42785 1

0 582 42784 3

0 582 46563 X

0 582 46564 8

0 582 46158 8

0 14 081562 7

0 582 42783 5

0 582 45146 9

0 582 45145 0

0 582 46901 5

0 14 081632 1

0 14 081656 9

0 582 44774 7

0 14 081619 4

0 582 42788 6

0 582 46566 4

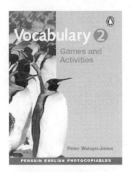

0 582 46565 6

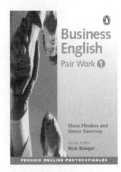

0 14 081680 1

0 14 081659 3

0 14 081662 3

 www.penguinenglish.com